THE PHOENIX BLUEPRINT

EMERGING STRONGER FROM
THE BLAZE OF HEALTHCARE

© **Copyright 2024 - All rights reserved.**

The content contained within this book may not be reproduced, duplicated, or transmitted without direct written permission from the author or the publisher.

Under no circumstances will any blame or legal responsibility be held against the publisher, or author, for any damages, reparation, or monetary loss due to the information contained within this book. Either directly or indirectly.

Legal Notice:

This book is copyright protected. This book is only for personal use. You cannot amend, distribute, sell, use, quote, or paraphrase any part, or the content within this book, without the consent of the author or publisher.

Disclaimer Notice:

By reading this document, the reader agrees that under no circumstances is the author responsible for any losses, direct or indirect, which are incurred as a result of the use of the information contained within this document, including, but not limited to, — errors, omissions, or inaccuracies.

TABLE OF CONTENTS

Introduction 1

Chapter 1: Feeling the Flames: Acknowledging Burnout's Grip....11

Chapter 2: Extinguishing the Flames: the RECHARGE Pathway to Overcoming Burnout Through Reclaiming Rest........................35

Chapter 3: Self-Study: Reflecting and Learning from the Flames .55

Chapter 4: Forging Fireproof Boundaries: Protecting Your Well-being 84

Chapter 5: Communicating Through the Smoke: Clear Messages for a Clearer Path 123

Chapter 6: Becoming a Lighthouse: Guiding Others Through the Fire... 151

Chapter 7: Battling the Blaze: Advocating for Change to Extinguish Systemic Burnout 171

Chapter 8: Igniting Your Creative Genius: Fanning the Flames of Innovation 189

Chapter 9: Gathering Around the Campfire: Fostering Community for Collective Resilience 216

Chapter 10: Rising from the Ashes: Embracing the Journey of Transformation... 237

Conclusion... 257

References... 259

INTRODUCTION

My story of burnout was of the insidious and sneaky variety, until it wasn't.

There is a saying about taking care of yourself or it will take care of you, or something like that. Basically, if you ignore stuff long enough, some major shit is going to go down.

For me, my moment of meltdown came during an intense family meeting in the Children's Hospital ICU. As a palliative care physician, it is my role to collaborate with the ICU team and family to clarify the goals of care and help shape the care plan into something that is aligned with the patient and family's goals while still medically sound. Our focus on palliative care is on the patient's suffering, with our aim to alleviate suffering as much as possible.

On this particular day, I was facing a very tough case. A young child who had severe heart disease and had been supported with a ventilator and ECMO machine (provides the functions of heart and lungs) for the past several weeks. The medical assessment of her condition was that it was irreversible, and she would never be able to survive without the support of these machines. The parents continued to hope for a miracle and were not ready to discuss discontinuing any of the support.

To further complicate the case, the parents were extremely focused on having the child awake so that they could interact, indicating some recognition that time was short even if they were otherwise unable to admit it. I, and most of the medical providers, felt that the child was suffering, not necessarily from the ongoing medical technology itself (although there were plenty of opinions about that) but from the undertreatment of her pain and other symptoms due to the desire for alertness. This alertness was never successfully achieved; if the child opened her eyes she was scared, grimacing, crying, and expressing distress in one way or another (she was, of course, unable to make any vocalizations due to the ventilator).

So here we were in this meeting trying to decide what to do. This is definitely a time you want your palliative care attending on their A game. The definition of success here is not necessarily either party "winning" or convincing the other they are right. The medical team frequently sees that as the goal—to convince the family their recommendations are correct and convince them to accept it. In palliative care we are often there as the counterbalance to this, to serve as the patient's advocate and make sure that the goals of the family are well understood by all before any decisions are made.

I wish I could tell you the story of some skillful and sophisticated communication and negotiation that went on that day. I wish this could be an illustration of how to thread the needle and find a solution that makes everyone happy. I have done that before in similarly challenging situations, that is what I do and I am good at it. But on this day, I stopped listening and I started yelling.

I yelled at the ICU attending, accusing him of not caring about this child's pain and underdosing her pain medication out of cowardice. I made bold claims about how "unacceptable" it was that this child was suffering in this way. When the ICU fellow was presenting the objective facts of the day (the heart rates, blood pressures, medication drip rates, etc.), I felt myself becoming more and more angry, feeding off her negative energy. The tone with which she read those numbers made it very clear that she was exhausted from caring for this patient day after day knowing that no progress was being made.

The bedside nurse was also indignant. I can only imagine the frustration and sadness she was feeling after three straight days of seeing this young child wince and cry every time she moved her, even slightly. The negative emotion in the room was palpable. And I caught it, big time. I was not the only one in that room that day who behaved unprofessionally. But I was the one who accused the family of not caring about their child. I was the one who said, "She is suffering because of you." I did not use those exact words, but that is what was conveyed.

Why did this happen? Because I was so fried I could not think. I was reactive. I heard the story of the child supported by machines and an ICU team who was failing to keep her properly medicated. I reacted, without further consideration. If I had been able to put even the slightest amount of daylight between stimulus and response, I may have asked a few questions. I may have come to understand that it was actually the parents who were requesting the lower doses, and I could have asked questions to better understand why that was. This is my procedure. This is what I do. It's not special magic, it's palliative care. And on this day, I failed to do my job. And I yelled.

I can't share the rest of the story. I don't know if the child remained on the machines, or if the parents eventually accepted the truth and agreed to discontinue them. I don't know if she continued to suffer or if the pain medication doses were eventually increased. I don't know any of this because after that meeting, the family requested that I no longer be involved in the care. Not only that, I was pulled off service and sent home for five weeks.

Disruptive physician. That is what we call it when a doctor's behavior is so egregious that they are disrupting the delivery of good care. That is what it looks like to be severely burned out.

This book describes my journey out. I didn't have a program to join or a community to lean on when I hit rock bottom. I studied and stumbled and found some guides. I found teachings that resonated and little by little, rebuilt my psychology and my nervous system to engage with the world differently.

Today, I consider myself burnout-proof. This is not because I spend my days on a beach attended to by a full household staff with millions of dollars in the bank. I currently work about 1.4 FTE all together, split between hospice for adults and children, pediatric hospitalist, and pediatric palliative care. My husband is also a physician, and we have two teenage daughters. Thankfully my health is good and my parents are living independently. I'd say this puts me somewhere in the middle of the challenge scale (not that there is one). The point is, my belief that I will never burn out again comes from my inner balance, not from my outside circumstances.

Everything I lay out in this book, everything that I had to do to claw my way out of the burnout hole and back to wholeness, has now created a version of me that is STRONG. I'm not done, for sure. One of the main skills I've developed is to embrace ongoing development.

My path to healing was through several modalities. I sought help from my physician initially, who referred me to a therapist who was incredibly beneficial in the early days when things were very acute. Then I found my way to yoga and an amazing teacher who showed me the full spectrum of the power of yoga, well beyond bendy postures. I also studied other philosophical traditions and took a deep dive into the world of positive psychology.

Throughout this book I will introduce concepts from yoga philosophy and stoicism that I find to be particularly relevant. I hope to inspire you to dive deeper into learning as you continue on your path of lifelong discovery. I know that many of us may roll our eyes when anyone mentions yoga as the antidote for burnout. This is primarily because yoga is thrown at us as a Band-Aid from administrations that don't want to do the hard work of systems improvement. The yoga I teach is a system for living. The bendy stuff on the mat is just one place to practice it all. So I ask that you keep an open mind as you come across a yoga concept. Try it on and see how it fits, don't just cast it away because you "hate it when they suggest yoga." I teach the art of discernment. I want you to cultivate a sense of what works for you and what doesn't so that you can craft your individual toolkit. Keep the beginner's mind and hold the possibility that this book contains new tools, and some of them may be for you.

I have a very personal stake in improving the US healthcare system. I am a doctor and I want good conditions for myself and the people whom I trained with and worked beside to work in. I am a consumer of healthcare. I have given birth and broken bones. I've gone through cancer treatments, and I have aging parents. I want there to be a wonderful world-class healthcare system to receive my loved ones and me when we need care. I believe it can be true.

The idea of a health system that works for everyone was initially developed in 2008 by IHI visionaries Donald Berwick, Thomas Nolan, and John Whittington. They proposed a "Triple Aim" as a way to guide healthcare systems and organizations in pursuing the overarching goals of improving the patient experience, improving population health, and reducing healthcare costs. It became a widely adopted model for healthcare improvement efforts.

In 2014, this model was expanded to the "Quadruple Aim" by adding a fourth goal of improving the well-being of healthcare workers. Most recently, in 2021, the "Quintuple Aim" was proposed by adding a fifth goal of advancing health equity. The innovation within this evolving model is the recognition that all five aims—patient experience, population health, cost reduction, provider well-being, and health equity—can and must be achieved simultaneously and synergistically. This rejects the notion that progress in one area must come at the expense of another. Instead, it presents a vision of a truly integrated and equitable healthcare system capable of delivering the best outcomes for all. As with any ambitious goal, such as putting a man on the moon, success will require a clear understanding of the intended endpoints and a relentless commitment to achieving them. The Quintuple Aim provides clarity of purpose to guide the transformation of our healthcare system.

We *have* to solve this problem. There really is no option. Are we just not going to have a healthcare system?! From where I sit, I can recognize the challenge and see that some very bright minds are needed to solve it. My role in the whole thing is to get everyone into a state in which they can have their most creative and innovative ideas. Think about it, you may be the one. You may have the next big idea that leads to major improvements in some sector of our crazy system. Right now you have too much burnout clouding your vision. My hope is that in reading this book and doing the work I lay out, you can clear that out and find your creative vision. Together we go farther.

Telling these stories feels urgent. The US healthcare system these days is like a raging fire that is set to burn to the ground. Every day going to work can feel like you are walking into the flames. I imagine this is how it must feel to be a firefighter, knowing that it is your job to walk into a fire every single day. Most of us, though, are more like that little cartoon dog sitting in the burning room saying everything is fine. But everything is not fine, and if we fail to acknowledge that we are entering a fire daily, we fail to protect ourselves and minimize the damage to healthcare workers. That's why I want to challenge you to be a phoenix or a firefighter, or both.

Firefighters train, firefighters prepare, firefighters have proper personal protective equipment, but at the end of the day, it's their job to go into a fire and come out again having saved as many people as possible. In a lot of ways this is exactly what we do as healthcare workers, except that the fire is metaphorical. The daily struggles faced by doctors, nurses, social workers and other healthcare professionals are emotional flames that can do as much damage. We need to determine what training, preparation, and emotional PPE we need to keep us safe through this firestorm.

The myth of the phoenix is of a bird that is destroyed by fire, and then rises from the ashes anew and afresh. In our metaphorical healthcare firestorm, the phoenix recognizes that the system may continue to burn, and putting out the fire may not be possible. The phoenix recognizes the power to rise from the ashes and will emerge as a stronger and renewed version of itself. The phoenix recognizes that the fire is part of its life cycle and that this cycle of burning and renewal is part of who it is. As we think about adopting the mentality of a phoenix, we will develop strategies to rise from this struggle and learn from it. The phoenix works with fire, not against it.

In both of these metaphors I am recognizing that dousing the fire completely is not something that is available at this time. I am all for systematic changes and improvements to our system. They are desperately needed, but the scope and the scale of the changes that are needed means that the course that it takes is unacceptably long to tolerate. You need to take action to protect yourself and get yourself into a wellness state now. You cannot wait until the fire has been extinguished to manage your own well-being. Healthcare professionals are leaving the field in droves.

So for all of those reasons, this book exists. This book is a guide on your personal path to whole, balanced living. Your personal path to becoming a firefighter or a phoenix or some combination thereof that allows you to keep going, that allows you to keep seeing patients and taking good care while admitting that you are a human being who has all of your own needs, emotions, thoughts, and insecurities.

This book will give you practical solutions to address your interactions with the fire beginning immediately. If we want to make systematic improvements, we need to get each individual into their highest and best state. We need every mind functioning optimally so that we can come up with creative solutions that will innovate the US healthcare system.

CHAPTER 1
FEELING THE FLAMES:
ACKNOWLEDGING BURNOUT'S GRIP

When I sat down to write this book, I tried to think back to when I first became burned out. My medical career is marked by two significant episodes of burnout. The ones that brought me to the brink of quitting, not just my career but life altogether. But as I thought more, I realized that I have lived in some version of burnout since high school. Only now, with clarity of vision and a completely transformed mindset, can I see that. When I was living it, I know I just thought it was normal. I was doing what everyone who was ambitious and high achieving did.

My first big crash came during my second year in medical school. Of course, med school started on a high. I was on the road to my dream, baby! Long hours dissecting the cadaver, memorizing every enzyme in the human body, and learning to recognize the microscopic appearance of every tissue were just steps on the path to the vision of the healer I knew I would be. I felt invincible, ready to heal, to make a difference. All that work I put in during high school and college was worth it. I was in medical school and life was going to be great.

Unfortunately, within one year I was already flaming out. The pressure to achieve begins early and the pace is relentless. Even before we see our first patient, we are overwhelmed with work. The only strategy offered is grit. Put your head down and do more, just do more. This builds on the habits we developed as undergrads, which were reinforced with the gift of this med school acceptance. The fire begins to feed itself. Worth becomes tied to productivity, grades, and performance on rounds. We enjoy the good feedback we get when we forgo sleep to study or to get in early and prep a few more charts.

More dangerous, I believe, is the narrative that gets ingrained early. The narrative of medicine being a calling and a privilege. Don't get me wrong, I firmly believe we should have passion for our work and gratitude for the opportunity. But this specialness comes with a cost.

You are a special being who has been chosen to receive the gift of caring for others. To honor this gift requires that you are willing to sacrifice everything. The patient comes first. You do not come first, your spouse, your children, your health, your happiness all come somewhere lower on the list. When you don the white coat, you are human no more. You are now something other. And whatever that other is, it does not include the opportunity to take a vacation, say no, or experience any human failings. No one told me I had to sacrifice my humanity to get my MD.

I wish I could say that my experience of burnout as a medical student was the catalyst that set me on the path to a more balanced life. It wasn't. I did manage to graduate (spoiler alert, you saw the MD on the cover of this book), but I didn't really learn anything about how to deal with stress or the systemic factors that led me here.

At the time, I didn't know to call it burnout and I certainly didn't know how or where to seek help. Thankfully, I did have some strong family support to at least keep my upright. I moved back in with my parents and spent nearly every day of spring semester under the covers wondering what I was going to do with my life because I clearly was not cut out to be a doctor. My mom is a nurse, so she also comes from the school of grit. *Just make it to graduation*. She went into battle mode to get me up and moving. Some days she would have to drive me to school because I couldn't quite figure out how to do that myself. Other days she would just let me be. My dad (pharmacist) made sure I was eating. Sleep was almost nonexistent, but at least I had a comfortable bed.

My memories of that time are hazy. I was living in a fog, completely untethered. I can't really say what I was thinking about during that time, but I am sure that thoughts of quitting school, running away, and even suicide crossed my mind. The fatigue was no longer just physical—it was emotional, mental, spiritual. Cynicism replaced compassion, and a sense of detachment took over. The very profession I loved and aspired to started to feel like a burden. By some miracle I got through to graduation, and this felt like success.

I moved out of state for residency, got married, and had a baby. Then moved again for fellowship and had another baby. Then I moved back closer to home and began practicing. Throughout all of this I kept pushing, kept grinding. It was the only skill I had so it became a badge of honor. Work 100 hours per week—ha, no problem! Take call every other night, of course, sleep isn't that important anyway. Increase your daily visits by 30 percent, what a fun challenge, I am up to it because I am amazingly efficient. All these narratives developed to buoy me through this incredible workload. I had no idea at the time how destructive this could become.

The Burnout Epidemic: A Raging Fire Consuming Healthcare

The US healthcare system finds itself smoldering in the flames of an insidious burnout crisis. What once was a bright calling to heal and provide compassionate care has been increasingly scorched by the unrelenting pressures of understaffing, overwork, and a bureaucracy that too often prioritizes financial gain over the well-being of its workforce. As the system strains and cracks under its own weight, an alarming exodus of physicians, nurses, and other healthcare professionals abandoning their roles hints at the severity of the blaze. This mass departure not only exacerbates existing shortages but robs patients of invaluable expertise and experience. With each skilled clinician who succumbs to the fires of burnout, the system loses another firefighter equipped to battle the inferno. If left unextinguished, these raging flames threaten to consume the very pillars of accessible, quality healthcare. Recognizing the depth of this crisis is the first step toward mobilizing urgently needed interventions and support systems to preserve the passion that first drew so many to this noble profession.

We enter this life knowing that there will be long hours, sick patients, lack of sleep, and a healthy dose of self-sacrifice. This has been true for generations, so why is the burnout getting worse?

The healthcare system has become a massive, unwieldy beast, the bureaucracy overwhelming, the pressure crushing. I believe that we are experiencing the meltdown of our current healthcare system. Every day we hear about staffing shortages, rising healthcare costs, and declining quality of care. Edward Deming, father of the quality movement, stated that "Every system is perfectly designed to get the results that it gets." From where I am sitting, it looks like the US healthcare system is a burnout machine.

This chapter is a mirror, a chance to see yourself reflected, and maybe, just maybe, to realize that you're not alone.

We're going to delve into understanding burnout, identifying its symptoms, and acknowledging its hold. We're going to examine the forces that contribute to burnout in healthcare, especially among women. We'll look at both the phoenix and the firefighter, two paradigms that can guide us through the flames.

Burnout has become epidemic in US healthcare. Even before the COVID-19 pandemic, the healthcare workforce was struggling. According to the surgeon general's report, 35-54 percent of nurses and physicians and 45-60 percent of medical students and residents reported symptoms of burnout. This is devastating for any attempts to try to salvage the healthcare system. Burned out clinicians are not operating at their best. Not surprisingly, this burnout is driving people out.

According to alarming reports, healthcare is facing a severe workforce crisis driven by burnout and unprecedented attrition. The 2023 Physicians Foundation survey revealed that 28 percent of physicians plan to retire within a year, up from 21 percent the previous year. Concerningly, 39 percent wouldn't pursue medicine again, and only 40 percent would recommend it as a career. A Mayo Clinic Proceedings study showed two in five physicians intend to reduce clinical hours over the next year—more than double the prior rate. The Association of American Medical Colleges projected a shortage of up to 124,000 physicians by 2034, exacerbated by early retirements.

The nursing workforce is equally imperiled. An Incredible Health survey found 23 percent of nurses plan to leave their current roles by year's end due to burnout, with 32 percent of those departing the field altogether. Staffing ratios remain a top driver of dissatisfaction. Despite over 200,000 new nursing graduates in 2021, this influx is outpaced by premature exits. Workforce data from 2021 showed that the total number of registered nurses in the US dropped by more than 100,000. There is a projected 10 percent shortage of registered nurses by 2026.

The comparisons starkly illustrate how an exodus of burned-out, seasoned professionals is creating untenable shortages that cannot be backfilled by the incoming pipeline alone. When so many leave their calling due to overwhelm, moral injury, and inability to deliver proper care, the entire system's capacity falters. The loss of so many skilled, seasoned nurses is creating significant experience and mentorship gaps that cannot be filled simply by the incoming graduates each year. Their early departures from the field are exacerbating already unfavorable staffing ratios, driving many to burn out and leave in the first place. Without interventions, this vicious cycle threatens to intensify the nursing shortage.

The high rates of physicians and nurses leaving the workforce due to burnout can have severe potential consequences across several areas:

Patient Care Quality

- Staffing shortages increase workloads on remaining staff, elevating risk of medical errors, delayed care, and negative patient outcomes
- Less experienced healthcare professionals stepping in can compromise quality of care, especially for complex cases
- Decreased patient satisfaction and eroded public trust in the healthcare system

Access to Care

- As physicians and nurses depart, it reduces overall healthcare capacity and availability of services
- This can increase wait times for appointments and procedures, delaying preventive and necessary care
- Rural and underserved areas may face even more limited access as providers congregate in urban centers

Rising Healthcare Costs

- Staff turnover creates additional hiring, training, and overtime expenses for healthcare facilities
- Shortages drive greater utilization of more expensive temporary staffing and travel nurses
- Increased costs are typically passed along to patients through higher medical bills and insurance premiums

Worsening Shortages

- A self-perpetuating cycle as more nurses and doctors leave due to excessive workloads created by existing vacancies
- This can create a "burnout contagion" effect as conditions deteriorate for those remaining

Brain Drain and Experience Deficits

- An exodus of advanced practice providers with decades of accumulated expertise and skill
- Potential impacts on medical education as fewer experienced preceptors to train incoming professionals

Public Health Emergencies

- Strained capacity can undermine pandemic/disaster response capabilities
- For example, nurse shortages already compromised COVID-19 testing and vaccination efforts

It's easy to see how these workforce dynamics can create a combustible feedback loop, accelerating burnout's scorching blaze. Just as a forest fire exponentially gains force with each tree it consumes, so does the dysfunction plaguing our healthcare system with every departed nurse or physician. As one care provider's exhaustion reaches the breaking point, the void leaves more patients channeled to colleagues already straining beneath excessive workloads—a brutal attrition cycle propagating more burned-out casualties.

Furthermore, the forces of corporate healthcare often appear to be actively pouring gasoline on these pyres. With profits and shareholder valuations as the uncompromising priority, staff well-being and sustainable working conditions seem an afterthought—merely kindling to be consumed in service of the insatiable bottom line. Squeezed to do furiously more with less, the very people shouldering healthcare's burden find themselves just more fuel sources omitted from the calculus.

As our experienced firefighters leave, the first lines of defense go with them. Our bygone systems of mutual support and uplift are crumbling as mentorship and camaraderie are left in the embers. All that remains are the greenest, most vulnerable nurses and doctors inhaling deep draughts of the toxins they were so unprepared to withstand. The scorched landscapes stretch from city to city, state to state—a uniformity of devastation where the fires of burnout have already torn through, ceding the embittered remains to catalyzing corporations' slash-and-burn expansion. Change is sorely needed, and it is hard to envision a way out. One thing is for sure, to find our way out, *we* need to be clear and well-functioning. I'm not certain that even if we recover our people, we can find a solution, but I am certain that we can't do it without it. The corporations fueling this blaze are not going to save us.

There are some bright spots. Some organizations have taken the initiative to improve, and we will discover some of the system-wide strategies that work throughout this book. But mostly this book is a guide for individual recovery. Hurt people hurt people and safe people save people. Continue reading if you are ready to transform from hurt to safe and begin saving people instead of perpetuating the cycle of hurt. You may have the next great idea that transforms the healthcare system. I want to help you unlock your creative genius and advocacy potential so that you can unleash it.

Recognizing Burnout

Okay, so maybe you are now thinking, maybe I am burned out. How do I know? There are several scales for measuring and quantifying burnout and for tracking well-being. Formal tools are best suited for tracking across time or in formal studies. For an individual person you can make a simple self-assessment by answering the questions below. Diagnosing burnout is only important so that you can get the right kind of help and support.

The term burnout has been used so often to refer to the experiences of healthcare workers that it seems to have almost become meaningless. People toss this out so casually these days, "Oh, I'm just a little crispy" or "I'm like a burned little potato chip," which can make you wonder if these people don't understand what burnout is or if they have become so numb and acclimated to the experience that they fail to recognize that gravity.

Burnout is known to be a severe and consequential condition. Burnout is associated with increased suicidal ideation.[8] Doctors experiencing burnout are twice as likely to make a medical error. And nurses experiencing burnout are twice as likely to leave their job.

One challenge in recognizing burnout is that it can be an ebb and flow process. We're not always burned out to the same degree. Some days, we feel slightly better—kind of okay-ish. There's still that constant background headache, brain fog, and muscle tightness lingering. But today, it took ten minutes instead of two to start snapping at people. And we actually connected with one out of the twenty-five patients we saw. Sounds like a downright fabulous day, right? But this is exactly the kind of false recovery that can trick us into thinking things aren't really that bad.

When we have a "not the worst day I've ever had" kind of reprieve, we get a little dopamine hit and collect just enough evidence to convince ourselves that maybe, just maybe, things are okay. Our brains are wired to protect us, and often what they want to protect us from is change itself. So we grasp at any reason to stay put with the status quo we know.

Have you heard the fable about the frog in the boiling water? If you toss a frog into a pot of violently boiling water, it will immediately jump out. But if you start with cool water and gradually heat it, the frog will remain and eventually get cooked to death. Now, being a city slicker,

I have no firsthand knowledge of how one might cook a frog. But I present this as a metaphor for the increasingly hot water many of us find ourselves in within the healthcare system. We may not feel like we're boiling because the temperature rose gradually over time. But if we fail to recognize our perilous situation and take action, we're going to get cooked.

The burnout triad consists of emotional exhaustion, cynicism, and lack of meaning or purpose. When clinicians are functioning in this state, this may look like anger toward patients, resentment of their job duties, cutting corners or doing the minimum amount necessary, or failing to connect with patients in a way that builds trust and connection. All of this is extremely detrimental to the clinician patient relationship and the quality of care provided. When burnout rates are high, safety and quality are low. For this reason, it is imperative that we do all that we can to address burnout.

Emotional exhaustion

Do you feel tired all the time, no matter how much you sleep? Do you feel like your soul is tired? Do you use sleep to avoid dealing with the stress of work or life? The moment that shook me to my core was my meltdown episode. I was sent home, not due to an illness, but because my spirit, my resolve, was nearing exhaustion. That day, it hit me like a freight train: I wasn't just tired, I was facing burnout. Burnout is a bit like a silent predator, creeping up on you when you least expect it. But it leaves signs in its wake, indicators that are too vital to ignore.

Remember the last time you had a fever? It was a sure sign that something was off in your body. Similarly, persistent exhaustion is a red flag for burnout. Are you constantly tired, irrespective of how much you sleep? Does your mind feel clouded, your body heavy, even after a full night's rest? Are you reaching for that fifth cup of coffee just to make it through the day? Or perhaps you're finding solace in sleep, using it as a safe harbor to escape from the pressures of your job.

Cynicism

Cynicism, or as I like to call it, the "distancing syndrome," is another telltale sign. You might feel detached from your work or your patients, like you're just going through the motions. Where once you felt empathy and connection, now there's a growing indifference. You might even catch yourself losing patience, becoming quick to snap, or zoning out when a patient shares their story.

Lack of meaning or purpose

What about purpose? Remember that fulfilling feeling when you saved a life or comforted a patient? But lately, have you found yourself questioning the very essence of your job? Do you ever catch yourself wondering, "What's the point?" You might even feel like a cog in the machine, questioning the impact of your work.

From a more personal perspective, when you are operating in a burned-out state, you are experiencing the physiologic effects of chronic stress. Chronic stress shows up in your body as headaches, abdominal pain, muscle tension, irritability, poor sleep. Over time this can lead to heart disease, dementia, stomach ulcers, and weight gain. Your relationships also suffer. Burnout doesn't just stay at work, it follows you home and gets in between every relationship that you have in your life. You may notice that you are more irritable with your kids, you have a shorter fuse. Perhaps you realize that you're distant from your spouse and not having the type of connection that you had in the past. Or maybe you notice that your attentiveness to your own health declines even further and further. The cynicism sets in at home too, and you begin to think *what's even the point*. This may lead you to turn to numbing activities like drugs, alcohol, food, or shopping.

Burnout Self-Assessment

This self-assessment incorporates elements from the Maslach Burnout Inventory and the Flourishing Scale, both of which are widely used in psychological studies for measuring burnout and well-being. For a more comprehensive assessment, consider completing the full versions of these instruments.

Remember, self-assessments are not definitive diagnoses but can serve as a starting point for recognizing and addressing burnout. If you're struggling, consider reaching out to a mental health professional for further support and guidance.

Please respond to each of the following statements based on how you've felt in the past week. Use the following scale:

1. - Never
2. - Rarely
3. - Sometimes
4. - Often
5. - Always

Cynicism:

1. I feel cynical about my work or the people I work with. 1 2 3 4 5
2. I feel indifferent toward the work that I do. 1 2 3 4 5
3. I feel detached from my colleagues or my work environment. 1 2 3 4 5
4. I find it hard to find meaning in my work. 1 2 3 4 5

Emotional Exhaustion:

1. I feel emotionally drained from my work. 1 2 3 4 5
2. I feel tired even when I wake up in the morning. 1 2 3 4 5
3. I feel burned out from my work. 1 2 3 4 5
4. I use sleep as an escape from my stress. 1 2 3 4 5

Personal Accomplishment and Engagement:

1. I feel satisfied with the work that I do. 5 4 3 2 1
2. I feel I make a significant impact through my work. 5 4 3 2 1
3. I feel connected with my colleagues and my work environment. 5 4 3 2 1
4. I feel energized by my work. 5 4 3 2 1

Scoring: Add up your score for each section. A higher score in the Cynicism and Emotional Exhaustion sections and a lower score in the Personal Accomplishment and Engagement section may indicate a higher level of burnout.

Remember, self-assessments are not definitive diagnoses but can serve as a starting point for recognizing and addressing burnout. If you're struggling, consider reaching out to a mental health professional for further support and guidance.

The Art of Navigating Change: Embracing Evolution for a Thriving Career

One thing we can learn from the business world is how to navigate change effectively. Entrepreneurs and corporate leaders understand that change is inevitable. Expecting an organization to thrive perpetually without updating systems or adapting messaging to meet evolving times is a surefire recipe for obsolescence—like becoming the next Blockbuster video, Palm Pilot, or MySpace.

While this is a book about burnout in healthcare, not business strategy, the lesson about embracing change is equally relevant. We must be ready to adapt and evolve. Everyone is clamoring for systemic changes in healthcare, but do we truly understand what that entails? For real change to occur, the people within the system must be willing to undergo personal changes themselves.

It's tempting to imagine that any changes will be tailored to our personal benefit, making our lives easier under a new idyllic "Sunshine and Rainbows Healthcare Plan." However, this can't possibly be true. With so many stakeholders harboring different ideas and priorities, any widespread change will inevitably leave some dissatisfied.

Even universally desired changes like safe staffing ratios and honoring promised vacation time will spark debates about implementation details. Should we have eight-hour or twelve-hour shifts? Specialized, decentralized care or a more comprehensive, slightly less specialized team-based approach? The possibilities for disagreement are endless.

The reality is that even when we get the systemic changes we've been clamoring for, not everyone will be happy with every aspect of the new reality. And that's why becoming an expert in navigating change may be the greatest asset you can cultivate for job satisfaction and career excellence in the years ahead. Those who can shift effortlessly and embrace evolution will thrive, while those resistant to change may struggle.

Reading this book and integrating the lessons provided will give you the very foundation you need to thrive for the long haul. I don't know what's coming. I do know that things will not stay the same. We never take the same breath twice.

Okay, so by now you are either in:

Camp 1 – nothing is going to change, I need to save myself.

or

Camp 2 – we need big changes; I need to be ready for them.

Great news, these steps are the recipe for success in either camp!

The Phoenix Blueprint: Awakening to a Life of Fulfillment

Burnout doesn't end at work. By continuing to live in a burned-out state, you are robbing yourself of the rich, fulfilling life you deserve. If you've been in this state for too long, you may have forgotten what a truly vibrant life feels like. Mere survival seems like enough, but deep down, you know it's not. Let me paint you a picture of inspiration, a vision of the Phoenix Blueprint—the antidote to burnout that will help you rise from the ashes and reclaim your passion.

Many healthcare professionals I've spoken with say their life is "fine" or "okay." They have the career, prestigious job, family, nice home, and vacations they envisioned as children. Yet something feels amiss. Despite achieving their goals, they're not truly happy. Why?

As healthcare workers, we witness the fragility of life—death, disease, and disability strip people of their functionality. We understand that our time is finite, which adds weight to the question: "Am I living a truly fulfilling life?"

There could be a few reasons for this disconnect. First, perhaps the blueprint you followed—the career, status, material possessions—doesn't align with your heart's deepest desires. You built the house according to the plan, but is it the right plan for you? It's time to check in with yourself and explore what truly matters.

Alternatively, life may have thrown curveballs, preventing you from fully realizing your initial blueprint. Loss, grief, challenges, or circumstances beyond your control could have altered your path. In chapter 3, we'll discuss how to focus on what's within your sphere of control and release what isn't. For now, the easiest action is gratitude.

As high achievers, we're always striving for more, optimizing, and leveling up—at the cost of appreciating what we've already accomplished. Take a moment to look around and thank yourself for your badassery in getting this far. But there's more to life than just surviving or achieving goals. The Phoenix Blueprint offers a path to rise from the ashes of burnout and reignite your passion for a truly rich, fulfilling life. In the coming chapters, we'll explore how to uncover your authentic desires, align your actions with your values, and soar to new heights of personal and professional fulfillment.

Facing my burnout was the hardest pill I had to swallow. It was a bitter realization, but it signaled the beginning of my transformation. I yearned to rise from my ashes, to reignite the phoenix within me, to be the healer I aspired to be. But before I could rebuild, I had to confront the reality of my burnout, feel the heat, and decide to emerge from the flames, renewed and resilient. So this is where our journey begins—acknowledging burnout and making the decision not to let it consume us.

The harsh reality is that the environment we operate in is unlikely to change overnight. Yes, there are conversations happening at the highest levels about system-wide changes, about making healthcare more sustainable, humane, and effective. But these are slow-moving, and while we wait, we continue to burn. It is vital that we remember, we are not helpless in this. We are the phoenixes. We are the firefighters. We possess the strength and resilience to rise above these flames. Our survival—and our capacity to thrive—depends on our ability to take proactive steps to acknowledge, address, and heal from burnout.

As we come to the end of this chapter, it's time for a deep breath. A pause. A moment to reflect on where we are in our personal journey. Have you seen yourself in my story?

Have you caught your reflection in the mirror of burnout? More importantly, are you ready to change your narrative?

The harsh reality of burnout is not to pull the curtains on our dreams but to trigger a transformation—a transformation from a burned-out shell to a thriving, resilient caregiver. It's a call to rewrite our narrative. The question is, are we ready to pick up the pen?

The following is a journaling exercise you may find beneficial as you work through this book and continue to understand more about yourself and your experience of burnout. In the next chapter we will discuss the importance of self-study and inward reflection. A daily habit of checking in with yourself using the template below will create a great foundation for you to do some deeper work. Enjoy!

Daily Reflection Exercise

Step 1: Recognize and Acknowledge Burnout

Take a moment to reflect on your day. Did you feel stressed, exhausted, or cynical toward work or life today? If yes, note down these feelings and situations that brought them up.

Step 2: Reflect and Journal Your Experiences

Write down any specific events or experiences from your day that you think contributed to these feelings. Reflecting on these instances can provide insights into triggers and patterns.

Step 3: Identify Your Stress Triggers

Can you identify any triggers that contributed to your stress or feelings of burnout today? These could be certain tasks, situations, or even individuals. Recognizing these triggers can help you develop strategies to manage them.

Step 4: Reach Out to Your Support System

Who did you reach out to today? How did it make you feel? Even if you didn't reach out to anyone today, note down any thoughts you have about reaching out to your support system.

Step 5: Create a Self-care Routine

Did you take out time for self-care today? If yes, jot down what you did and how it made you feel. If not, plan one self-care activity for tomorrow and note it down.

Step 6: Closing Thoughts

Write down any other thoughts, reflections, or feelings about your day here. Remember, no thought or feeling is insignificant when it comes to managing burnout.

"Vulnerability is not winning or losing; it's having the courage to show up and be seen when we have no control over the outcome."

- Brené Brown

CHAPTER 2
EXTINGUISHING THE FLAMES:
THE RECHARGE PATHWAY TO OVERCOMING BURNOUT THROUGH RECLAIMING REST

Now that we have recognized how pervasive burnout can be and how damaging it is, let's start with a truth-telling moment. Raise your hand if you have ever hoped for a cancer diagnosis (or other serious health condition) so that you could get a break from work.

Truth be told, that's exactly where I found myself when I got the call during rounds that my routine mammogram had detected an abnormal finding, requiring a biopsy. As a healthcare professional myself, I had no clue what to do next. As much as I panicked that I might have cancer, part of me was fantasizing about what it might be like to be on medical leave. Not because I wanted to be sick, but because it felt like the only way I'd give myself permission for true rest and renewal.

I now can see that I was exhausted and running on empty. Because of the hustle mentality and grit and grind work ethic that had been ingrained throughout my medical training, I did not believe that I deserved rest unless it was a life-threatening situation. Every time I thought about calling in sick, I had flashbacks to the days of dragging an IV pole on rounds or vomiting on my attending's shoes because staying home was just not an option. Everyone I know has stories like this, we push our bodies and consider it part of being a good doctor.

The culture of overwork and glorified productivity has allowed the flames of burnout to rage out of control in healthcare. One that celebrates self-sacrifice at the expense of human well-being. Humans are not made to constantly grind. We need to rest in order to rise.

Rather than feeding those merciless flames with the worn-out fuel of self-criticism and over-giving, we can learn to guard our inner light through cycles of meaningful work followed by complete, guilt-free renewal.

So I invite you to allow these words and practices to awaken the phoenix within you. To boldly claim your need for rest and balance as the most compassionate act. Just as firefighters have strict rest requirements, so must those battling the blaze of a broken system.

The RECHARGE Pathway

Many of these principles are derived from yogic philosophy outlined in the classical yoga text called the Yoga Sutras of Patanjali. At the core of the yogic philosophy are the Yamas and Niyamas—guideposts illuminating the attitudes and behaviors that foster flourishing for individuals and society.

The Yamas are the "restraints" or moral virtues centered on our relationship with the external world. Ahimsa (non-violence) teaches reverence for all life. Satya (truthfulness) aligns our thoughts, words and deeds. Asteya (non-stealing) promotes taking only what is truly ours. Brahmacharya (moderation) balances our efforts and desires. And aparigraha (non-possessiveness) liberates us from the rat race of materialism.

The Niyamas are the "observances" governing our inner world and self-discipline. Saucha (purity) clears our bodies and minds of toxins. Santosha (contentment) helps us accept what flows rather than grasping. Tapas (discipline) burns away our limiting beliefs. Svadhyaya (self-study) leads to sacred self-awareness. And Ishvara pranidhana (surrender) aligns us with a higher power.

By following these ethical principles as guideposts, we create the foundations for true personal renewal. We become empowered to release toxic patterns, realign our values, and open to our most vibrant potential as human beings. For the purposes of this model, I am calling this highest potential self the *Fireborn Human.*

The RECHARGE pathway outlines these time-honored principles and practices in a way that is accessible for our modern lives.

R – Rest

When my mammogram detected abnormal findings requiring multiple biopsies, lumpectomies, and radiation treatment, I was inadvertently gifted with a great lesson in true rest. My initial instinct (once the initial shock cleared) was to "power through" these various treatments with the efficiency and drive I applied to everything else in life. But the universe had a few tricks up its sleeve to make sure I got the rest I needed.

On my first lumpectomy surgery I had a complication that led to a severe corneal abrasion. While not life-threatening, it hurt like hell and limited me from using my eyes for forty-eight hours. This was a real opportunity to slow down—couldn't move much because the boobs hurt, couldn't watch TV or read, just slept or listened to music and let the house run itself. Then there was the second biopsy that was supposed to be a quick "rule out" since all the cancer had been resected already. Well, not only did this one find more abnormal cells, but I also had so much bleeding I looked like I had been shot by the time I got home. My 32D T-shirt bra had done its best but that modesty pad is not really super absorbent.

While not the ideal circumstances, these experiences etched a profound realization—that real rest is non-negotiable for surviving life's inevitable fires. Not just physical sleep, but giving your body and mind extended pauses to heal and recalibrate. Without this rejuvenating rhythm, we burn out.

E – Ease

The path of ease means no more frantic forcing or white-knuckling your way through life. It's making life energy-efficient by aligning with natural, flowing cycles rather than always blazing against the current. For overachievers, this may feel counterintuitive, but ease actuates the force of yin—embodying purposeful pause, simplicity, and letting go where appropriate.

Finding ease means not fighting it. Instead of being upset that you can't read or work on your computer, embrace the opportunity to just get some extra sleep. Allow other people to help you. You are likely surrounded by people who love you and have been waiting for you to say you need something. Find ease by seeing your request as an invitation. Think about how happy it makes you to help someone else—don't you want to allow that joy in others? Don't fight it, find ease.

Yes, this is a skill that many of us are not fully developed in. We seem to be overdeveloped in making everything as difficult as possible. One question I always ask myself is, "What if it was easy?" What if it was easy to sit in the dark for two days? What if it was easy to sit still while the radiology resident holds pressure on your biopsy site?

What if it was easy to not jump ahead to "what if" and focus on what is?

The yogic principle of aparigraha means non-grasping. We need to release our tendency to hoard or forcefully control people and situations beyond our radius. Understanding and applying this principle encourages us to loosen our grip. Try this practice to make this concept tangible.

Envision tightly clenching your fists, allowing the tensions of grasping and attachment to arise. Then gradually relax your grip, opening your hands and breathing out any residual tightness. Let this experience be your reminder to open to ease.

C – Compassion

Ahimsa, the yogic tenet of non-violence, must be applied inwardly before we can embody it outwardly. Often we are our own harshest critics, berating ourselves for perceived flaws and failures. There I was, secretly hoping for a cancer diagnosis just to get a sanctioned break. How could I have deprived myself of basic human compassion to that extent? Yet that moment revealed how normalized burnout culture had become—where we berate ourselves mercilessly for any need, denying our humanity in service of toxic hustle.

The Fireborn Human path rejects this violence. It embraces radical self-compassion—nurturing rather than narcissistic. From this loving space, you can heal and restore. You can forgive yourself and make sustainable changes. Self-compassion is the font allowing you to finally replenish.

To cultivate self-compassion, try this exercise: Bring to mind a challenging situation you've judged yourself harshly for. See yourself dealing with this difficulty through a lens of kindness—soothing your anguished inner child rather than attacking. What words of warmth and reassurance would you offer? Let them wash over your being.

H – Harmony

When we live in burnout we are in dissonance. Things are chaotic and out of sync. The Fireborn Human reclaims a more harmonious flow by attuning to natural cycles—body clock patterns, seasonal flows, periods of intense effort balanced by extended rejuvenation.

As I experienced the unpredictable delays and deviations from my expected treatment timelines, I faced a choice: fight the lack of order and control or surrender to harmonizing with reality as it unfolded. This became an education in finding this rhythm.

Notice when your workload is out of sync with these organic rhythms, leading to force and struggle. Can you spot any unnecessary resistance causing discord? Build in rejuvenating pauses between periods of intense effort. Small adjustments to realign with nature's cadences can significantly boost your harmony.

A – Awareness

Without the present moment awareness to truly feel the impact of burnout on your mind and body, the wake-up calls go unheeded. You remain checked out, disconnected, running solely on fumes and muscle memory.

It was only by directly experiencing my physical limits through procedures like radiation—the skin irritations, the accumulating fatigue, the "stop" signals—that I could no longer ignore the fierce importance of tuning in. Of paying exquisite attention to what my soul needed to thrive once again.

Amid the relentless mental chatter and outward busyness, it's easy to lose touch with the present moment—where your true power resides.

This simple conscious breathing exercise can awaken awareness: Take a long, deep inhale, expanding your belly. Then slow exhale through the nostrils. During each inhalation, feel the aliveness moving through your body. On the exhalations, relinquish any mental burdens. Continue this rhythmic attunement to breath for a minute or two daily to recharge presence.

R – Renew

Beyond rest, we require sanctuaries—designated practices that facilitate continual rejuvenation of our mind, body and spirit. What nurtures and fills your tanks?

Develop a personal renewal plan selecting from options like meditation, creative projects, time in nature, physical practices, or anything that allows you to blossom. Schedule these growth facilitators as you would other priorities to recharge vitality.

I have three core practices that I incorporate. Morning meditation, a lunch break ritual that involves mindful eating and some sort of movement, and a weekly digital detox evening. Along with attention to my sleep routine, nutrition plan, and exercise routine, these practices form the foundation of my overall well-being.

Renewal practices broadcast new neural pathways that allow us to become stronger and more grounded.

G – Gratitude

Gratitude is the antidote to fear. And living in fear will always keep the filter of scarcity, depletion, and frantic striving in place. True joy can emerge when you can move past scarcity and your constant focus on what is wrong.

Some of my most poignant memories from my time in treatment came from the surprise rituals of community and caring that occurred during my radiation visits. Swapping inspirational sayings and candies with the other patients became small ceremonies reminding me to cherish each day's offerings. The daily smile from the guy at the front desk brightened my mood and was a reminder that I also have the opportunity to brighten the day for others. Even the recognition that I was not the sickest person there inspired me to be grateful for all the ways that I was still healthy.

Gratitude grounded me in the truth that even in life's darkest valleys, there are still unmissable gifts. I am grateful for the experience of having been a patient. I see the gratitude for life's small gifts reflected in my patients every day. The Fireborn Human experiences gratitude for their own experiences and gifts and is also amplified in witnessing and sharing the gratitude in others.

The principle of santosha (contentment) is an antidote to the endless grasping, aversion and lack that fuels our cultural burnout. To foster more santosha, try a daily gratitude journal: In the morning, set an intention to truly savor the small pleasures throughout your day. In the evening, record three to five specific moments, interactions or gifts you felt grateful for, allowing yourself to fully reexperience that appreciation.

E - Embrace Impermanence

For achievement-driven personalities, there can be a relentless pursuit of permanence—doing whatever it takes to hold on to success, health, and our carefully constructed identities. But as I saw through the unpredictable bumps in my treatment road, that white-knuckle grasp is an illusion.

There were constant reminders that true permanence is impossible, no matter how tightly we cling. The Fireborn Human develops the fluid wisdom to embrace this impermanence—to soften and let each experience unfurl and pass without resistance. It's the path of constant becoming.

A simple mantra like "This too shall pass" can help us remember the transient nature of every experience, transcending our rigid attachments.

This RECHARGE framework is your path of reclamation. A time-proven methodology to extinguish the cultural flames of burnout with radical, sustainable self-renewal practices. No more bone-deep exhaustion. No more admiring self-destruction as noble currency.

Breaking the Busyness Cycle

When we are stuck in the burnout cycle, we believe that the way out is by working more. Stay longer, do a bit more, go the extra mile…somehow we convince ourselves that if we complete just one more task, or "lean in" and get the team over this next hurdle, we will magically feel so much better. Well-intentioned leaders reward us for these behaviors and encourage us to "dig deep" and "develop more resiliency" to get through the tough days.

The trouble is, we have been in tough days for months going on years going on decades. Strategies that were developed to mitigate a temporary crisis are now being deployed day after day after day. This leaves you in a constant state of depletion and overwhelm. What you really need is rest. Deep, meaningful rest.

The culture of overwork is a pervasive and troubling phenomenon that has become deeply embedded in many modern workplaces and societies. It's a mindset that glorifies long hours, constant hustle, and a blurring of boundaries between work and personal life. Recognizing this as a pervasive aspect of life in modern times is an important step in taking action against it. In medical settings, this culture is heightened by the high-achieving personality of people who tend to go into medicine as well as the training systems that normalize extremely long hours and few breaks.

Here are some of the ways this shows up in healthcare careers:

- Glorification of Busyness: There's a strange badge of honor associated with being perpetually "busy" and overwhelmed with work. Overwork is seen as a virtue, a sign of dedication and importance rather than a dangerous imbalance.
- Feast or Famine Cycles: Many workplaces promote cycles of intense "binge working" followed by post-call lulls. This inconsistent workload makes it hard to establish sustainable rhythms and reinforces habits of overexertion.
- Lack of True Downtime: Even when not at the hospital or clinic, people remain tethered to their devices and an expectation of constant availability and responsiveness. True uninterrupted downtime to recharge is scarce.

- Competitive Overwork: Peers subtly compete and one-up each other with tales of late nights, missed weekends, and personal sacrifices made for the job, creating a spiral of overwork.
- Inadequate Boundaries: There's a lack of policies and cultural norms promoting work-life balance boundaries. The implicit expectation is that work scales infinitely with unlimited demands.
- Lack of Recovery Support: Few workplaces actively promote recovery practices like vacations, mental health days, or resources for managing stress and burnout. Powering through is the norm.
- Fear-Based Motivators: Much overwork is driven by fear—fear of being seen as replaceable, fear of missing opportunities, fear of underdelivering on ever-increasing expectations.

Ultimately, the overwork culture stems from flawed definitions of productivity that value "busyness" over sustainably paced and healthy achievement. It's a workplace culture badly in need of a philosophical reset.

Rest is Not Lazy

Instead of asking ourselves if we have done enough work to earn our rest. We should ask ourselves, have we rested enough to do our best work.

This productivity trap is so ingrained in American culture and medical culture that it can be very hard to overcome. We have internalized this now, so even if we don't have a boss or supervisor looking over our shoulder saying "do more," we feel it ourselves. We push ourselves to add one more patient, make a few more phone calls, read another journal article (or write one), pick up another shift, or stay a few hours longer. Now there are, of course, multiple drivers of these behaviors. But our fundamental belief that we do not deserve to rest until all the work is done is a big one. The other is a fundamental belief that rest equals laziness. We attach worth to working and have very narrow definitions about what constitutes work.

This sets up a system in which no one can succeed. All the work will never be done. New tasks and needs are created faster than we can complete them. This is why the healthcare system is in meltdown. But the solution for you can't be to say, "Well I will do more, faster, and take less rest so that this problem can get solved." That strategy reminds me of the *I Love Lucy* episode, "Job Switching", where Lucy and Ethel are working at the chocolate factory and trying to keep up as the belt goes faster and faster. It makes for amazing physical comedy, but is a terrible strategy for creating a sustainable career.

Embrace rest as part of your life. Know that you are worthy no matter how much you do. If you have a day where you lie around in your PJs sipping tea, reading fun books, and watching TV—that is a highly productive and successful day. On the other hand, a day at work "busy" answering emails and calls, restacking papers, and attending ineffective meetings could be a very unproductive day because it doesn't bring you closer to your goals.

It is all about intention, values, and the goals you have.

Burnout and the Power of Time Blocking

To get people in the habit of intentional rest, I like to use a time blocking strategy and schedule time for rest. Here's the technique. This is an amazing time management strategy overall, but for right now we are not focused on learning how to do more stuff. We are going to focus on scheduling time for rest.

Time blocking is a method that involves dividing one's day into blocks of time, with each block dedicated to a specific task or activity. Instead of operating with a simple to-do list, where tasks might take longer than expected and bleed into one another, time blocking allows for clear start and end times. This method provides structure to the day and ensures that there's a designated period for each activity, be it work, exercise, leisure, or rest. By visually representing one's day or week, individuals can ensure a more balanced distribution of time and energy.

Scheduling Rest: An Essential Block

Rest isn't just the absence of work; it's an active and vital process that rejuvenates the mind and body. Unfortunately, in our hustle-centric culture, rest often gets deprioritized. However, by using time blocking, one can make rest a non-negotiable part of the schedule. Just as one might block off an hour for a meeting or a project, it's equally crucial to block off time for relaxation, be it a twenty-minute power nap, an hour-long walk, or an evening without screens. When rest becomes a scheduled part of one's day, it takes on the same importance as any work task, reinforcing its significance in maintaining our well-being.

The Mental Clarity Gained from Scheduled Rest

Time blocking rest doesn't just mitigate burnout; it also improves overall performance. When the brain is given time to recharge, it can process information more effectively, enhance creativity, and boost problem-solving skills. A well-rested mind is sharper, more focused, and can tackle tasks with greater efficiency. By setting aside dedicated blocks for rest, one ensures that these rejuvenating breaks are interspersed throughout the day, preventing the buildup of stress and mental fatigue.

Embracing Time Blocking for a Holistic Life

The battle against burnout is ongoing, but strategies like time blocking provide tangible tools to help individuals navigate their busy lives. By intentionally scheduling rest and valuing it on par with other tasks, one sends a powerful message about its importance. It's an acknowledgment that to be truly productive and fulfilled, we must respect our need for pauses and rejuvenation. By integrating time blocking into daily routines, one doesn't just manage time better but also carves out the essential space to breathe, refresh, and ultimately thrive amid life's demands.

Block Time for Sleep

I have recently come to learn a lot more about sleep and have been convinced that it is the #1 most important aspect of our well-being. Neuroscientist Matthew Walker summarizes many of the key benefits of sleep in his book *Why We Sleep*. I have included a few of the key learnings below. I hope that some of this evidence convinces you that adequate sleep is the foundation for every other goal you may have. If you do nothing else, get some sleep! Aim to block off seven to nine hours per day of "sleep opportunity," which is the time you are in bed preparing for sleep and sleeping.

- The Impact of Sleep on Learning and Memory: Sleep plays a crucial role in consolidating memories and enhancing cognitive abilities, with REM sleep boosting problem-solving skills and creativity; prioritizing quality sleep can significantly improve your capacity for learning and making sound decisions.
- Sleep and Physical Health: Lack of sleep is a recipe for numerous health issues, as it increases the risk of heart disease, obesity, a weakened immune system, and even DNA damage; getting sufficient, restorative sleep is paramount for maintaining physical well-being.
- Sleep and Mental Health: Sleep deprivation can exacerbate mental health conditions like anxiety and depression, while adequate sleep promotes

emotional regulation and overall psychological health; prioritizing sleep should be a key component of any mental health regimen.
- Sleep Across the Lifespan: Sleep needs and patterns vary across different life stages, and failing to meet these needs can have detrimental effects on development, cognition, and overall health; understanding and accommodating these changing sleep requirements is essential for thriving at any age.
- The Role of Dreams: Dreams serve important functions in emotional processing, problem-solving, and creativity; by allowing for quality dream sleep, you can harness the powerful benefits of this often-overlooked cognitive state.
- Strategies for Healthy Sleep: Cultivating healthy sleep habits is a skill that can be learned and optimized through practical strategies outlined in Walker's book; investing time in developing a personalized sleep routine can pay dividends in overall well-being.

Block Time for Non-sleep Rest

Geez, Emma, first you make me take time for seven to nine hours of sleep a day, and now you want me to rest even more? Yes, our brains and bodies benefit from all types of rest. The two I want to introduce now are play and meditation.

Play is the general term assigned to anything that we do without a specific purpose. Just letting go and having fun. Or letting something not be so serious. We know that play is essential for brain development in children, why have we forgotten that it is good for adults too?

Meditation is a resting state of the mind that is not asleep. We will learn more about meditation and the power of mindfulness in upcoming chapters. Shift your perspective to see this as a gift to yourself.

Once you become familiar with the time blocking technique, you can turbo charge this strategy with additional time management and prioritization skills. Two great books on this topic are *Getting Things Done* by David Allen and *Indistractable* by Nir Eyal. Check out my website for more in-depth descriptions of these strategies as you get deeper into your personal development journey.

Try out time blocking today. Be sure to schedule some time for rest and for self-reflection. In the next chapter, we will learn all about the importance of looking inward and the transformative power it can have.

"Rest and self-care are so important. When you take time to replenish your spirit, it allows you to serve others from the overflow."

- Zig Ziglar

CHAPTER 3
SELF-STUDY:
REFLECTING AND LEARNING FROM THE FLAMES

I have the life of my dreams. I work in a few roles that all weave together and allow me to have my perfect day at work every day. I have time to exercise, write, create, play, and nurture important relationships. My day includes hard work and rest. And my job allows me to support myself and my family in a wonderful lifestyle we enjoy greatly. You can have it too if you are just willing to self-study.

Now that we have learned to rest, we need to learn to look inward and embrace self-study. In yogic tradition this is called Svadyaya (fun word, right?). Svadyaya is one of the Niyamas, those yogic rules for living that we learned about in chapter 2. In the yogic tradition the observance of self-study leads to *sacred self-awareness.* I don't know about you, but if I'm trying to navigate a firestorm and figure out the best way to become a firefighter or a phoenix, I would love to have as much sacred self-awareness as possible!

Self-study involves exploring various aspects of yourself at multiple levels. At the surface, it entails understanding your preferences, natural rhythms, personal needs, and general tendencies. Delving deeper, self-study helps you identify your strengths, values, and a framework for decision-making, which can enhance your engagement and productivity in work. Ultimately, the deepest level of self-study involves cultivating a habit of mindfulness—observing your thoughts and emotions with dispassionate objectivity. By developing a system to interact with your inner experiences consciously, you can gain profound self-awareness and personal growth.

Let's start at the surface level. Commit to paying attention and becoming intimately familiar with your daily patterns, preferences, and needs. Pay close attention to when you feel most energetic and productive throughout the day—are you a morning person or a night owl? What types of activities and environments allow you to focus best? Identify the self-care practices that help you recharge, whether it's getting enough sleep, exercising regularly, or taking breaks for leisure activities.

Notice your eating habits and how different foods affect your energy levels and mood. Explore your interests and hobbies outside of work; these can provide important insights into your natural inclinations and sources of joy. By attuning to these surface-level aspects of yourself, you can start structuring your days, weeks, and months in alignment with your unique rhythms and tendencies, optimizing your well-being and performance.

One tool to help see how you are currently spending your time is the time audit. Simply watching (and writing down) what you are doing every hour for a few days in a week can be illuminating. A time audit worksheet can be found on our website. Feel free to print out as many copies as you need. Or download the template and complete it electronically.

As you learn more about your unique strengths and your prioritized values, you will use your time audit to see if where you are spending your time aligns with the things you consider most important. As I was pulling myself out of burnout and trying to draw myself a map to a better future, this is exactly where I started. I spent years dreading going to work. I was inspired by the kind of work I did (pediatric palliative care and oncology) but the actual doing of it was just draining. I would complain nonstop about all the things that were wrong with my job. Every day I had a rant about "I would really love this job, if only…" One day I decided to stop complaining and actually write down all the things that came after "if only." What would make this the perfect job? What would make me happy?

At its most basic, this exercise has you map out each hour of the day and just watch what you are doing. After a few days you will have a sense for how you spend your time.

Then you can map this to the various domains or goals you have for yourself and see if it lines up or not. Mapping activities to domains doesn't have to be complicated. You just assign whatever you were doing to some meaning or reason you were doing it.

I suggest that you do it for a couple of days, because not every day for us is the same. This exercise is incredibly value as an initial practice of self-study, because a lot of times, we might make a values-based goal strategy and then realize we're actually spending a lot of time doing other things. And that's where we have to come back, reevaluate, and recognize this is a great opportunity to set boundaries!

As you're working through thinking about all this, learning more about how you spend your time and attention, I want to offer one additional prompt: *what happens if you don't do it?*

Be fierce for yourself. Because when we're thinking about time and attention, there are some things that are really important. And then there are some things that feel important. So I want you to apply this question to them to figure out if they really are. If the answer to this question is *someone might not like me*, we need to get over that real fast! However, if the answer is that some very important relationship will be damaged in some way, that's a good answer.

Things that are important to our most important people are our priorities. But if it's some peripheral character who's probably been sort of abusing or taking advantage of you, let me give you permission to allow them to be upset with you or may not like you. It is okay.

The real answer to this question a lot of times is *nothing*. Absolutely nothing, good or bad, will happen if you don't do that thing. We have wrapped ourselves up in our stories so tightly we can't even realize how insignificant a lot of our stuff is.

I needed to take several weeks out of work due to medical issues. I didn't go to work, answer emails, do phone calls. Nothing for several weeks. And not a lot had happened. Obviously, the clinical work needed to be covered. But all of those emails that we feel urgently need to be answered? All those pressures we feel to write this or do this or do that, or people are somehow going to forget who you are, or you're going to lose your reputation, or something's going to happen. Most of the time, that doesn't happen. So that was a transformative experience for me to see that when I stopped doing all the things that I thought were so important for a while, nothing bad happened.

Most of the people didn't know that I was on medical leave. All they knew was their email wasn't getting answered. So it's not that people were giving me extra grace because I was having surgery. Some people knew, and those were the people who covered my clinical schedule. But most of the people didn't know. They just got that out-of-office message that I was going to be unavailable for a few weeks, and that was it. This made me realize that I could put up an out-of-office message *anytime I want*.

Strengths and Values

When I work with clients either one-on-one or in teams, I always start with an inventory of their strengths. Focusing on our strengths first empowers us and makes it easier for us to make the changes needed to lead more fulfilling and effective lives. A strengths-based approach encourages people to name and use their innate talents, which enhances confidence. Figuring out which strengths you are naturally high in is a great step in diving deeper into your self-study.

Here are some practical steps you can take to name and use your core strengths:

1. Take a strengths assessment: Complete the VIA Strengths Inventory or another reputable strengths assessment to gain insights into your top strengths. Find a free link on our website.
2. Reflect on past successes: Think about times when you felt most energized, engaged, and effective. What strengths were you using in those situations?
3. Seek feedback from others: Ask trusted friends, family members, or colleagues what they perceive as your greatest strengths and when they've seen you at your best.

4. Analyze your interests and passions: Find activities or topics that naturally draw your attention and motivate you. These often align with your strengths.
5. Set strengths-based goals: Craft personal and professional goals that allow you to apply and develop your core strengths.
6. Redesign your roles and responsibilities: Where possible, adjust your work or life roles to better suit your strengths. Delegate or minimize tasks that drain your energy.
7. Practice using your strengths in new ways: Stretch yourself by applying your strengths to novel situations or challenges. This builds confidence and mastery.
8. Partner with others who have complementary strengths: Collaborate with individuals whose strengths balance or supplement your own, creating synergy and mutual growth.
9. Keep a strengths journal: Regularly reflect on and record how you're using your strengths, noting successes, insights, and areas for further development.
10. Continuously learn and refine: Stay committed to understanding and applying your strengths more effectively over time. Read, attend workshops, or seek mentorship to deepen your strengths-based practice.

By taking these proactive steps, you will gain greater self-awareness and begin to intentionally harness your unique capabilities. In future chapters, we will consider how this strengths-based lens can be used to improve relationships and build community.

Values are the enduring beliefs, principles, or standards that guide an individual's behavior, attitudes, and choices. Values are deeply personal and can shape how we perceive the world, interact with others, and find meaning and purpose in our lives and work. Imagine your core values as the trunk of a mighty oak tree. Deeply rooted beliefs, principles, and standards that define who we are at our core. Just as an oak tree's trunk is solid and unchanging, our fundamental values tend to be stable and enduring over time.

However, the branches, leaves, and smaller details of the tree are more flexible and changeable. These components can represent our habits, preferences, styles, and superficial aspects of our lives that may shift and adapt based on circumstances, seasons, or personal growth. The leaves might fall off and regrow in different patterns each year, just as our habits and tastes can change regularly. The branches might bend or break in storms, resembling how we change our styles or behaviors in response to challenges or transitions. But through it all, the trunk—our core values—stays firmly rooted and unwavering.

Our deepest values tend to be quite stable once we reach adulthood. Transformative experiences such as becoming a parent or suffering a major loss may shift our values, but for the most part they are steady as the oak's trunk.

Understanding our core values is a very powerful part of knowing ourselves. Our goal for flourishing in life is to have the greatest degree of alignment between our core values and our actions.

The following values clarification exercise is designed to help you identify and reflect on your core values. Our core values can serve as a yardstick or touchstone for us to gain better understanding of our decision-making process.

Reflect on the list of values below and identify the values that truly resonate with you. The goal is to stay open and curious so that you can find your personal core values, not based on societal expectations or ideals. This list is not exhaustive, feel free to add if there are other things you find useful.

64 | The Phoenix Blueprint

Values List

Authenticity	Growth	Perseverance
Balance	Harmony	Personal Growth
Community	Health Honesty	Respect
Compassion	Honor Humility	Responsibility
Continuous	Independence	Risk-Taking
Learning	Integrity	Security
Courage	Joy	Self-Awareness
Creativity	Justice	Self-Expression
Curiosity	Kindness	Service
Discipline	Knowledge	Simplicity
Equality	Leadership	Spirituality
Excellence	Loyalty	Stability
Fairness	Love	Success
Family	Mindfulness	Teamwork
Freedom	Optimism	Trust
Friendship	Peace	Wisdom
Gratitude		

Use the following prompts to help you dive even deeper and further clarify which values you hold most dear.

1. Value ranking: Rank your top 5-10 values in order of importance and explain why you prioritized them in that way.

2. Value scenarios: Consider one or more of the following scenarios and reflect on how the values you prioritized could guide your decision making. Which value touchstones make the decision feel easiest? What values may be in tension in each scenario? How would you

decide which one "wins" if two of your priority values conflict with each other?

- Balancing patient needs with personal boundaries: You have a patient who frequently calls after hours with nonurgent concerns, disrupting your personal time. How do you balance providing quality care with maintaining healthy boundaries and work-life balance? What values come into play?
- Allocation of limited resources: There is a shortage of a life-saving medication, and you must decide how to allocate the limited supply among several critically ill patients. What values guide your decision-making process in this ethically complex situation?
- Navigating hierarchies and power dynamics: You witness a senior colleague belittling or mistreating a junior staff member. Do you speak up, even though it could jeopardize your working relationship or career prospects? What values influence your choice?
- Honesty and truth-telling: A patient asks you directly about their prognosis, but their family has requested that you withhold certain details. Do you prioritize honesty and patient autonomy or respect the family's wishes? How do your values shape this decision?
- Professional integrity and whistleblowing: You become aware of unethical or dangerous practices occurring within your healthcare organization. Do you risk your job and reputation to report these issues externally or remain silent to protect your career? What values weigh on this choice?

- Personal beliefs and professional obligations: You are asked to provide a medical service or treatment that conflicts with your personal moral or religious beliefs. How do you reconcile your professional duties with your personal value system?
- Prioritizing self-care: You are exhausted and burning out, but your team is already short-staffed. Do you prioritize your own well-being by taking time off, or do you push through to support your colleagues and patients, potentially at the expense of your mental health?

3. Value alignment: Consider how well your current life and career align with your stated values. Where do they see congruence or disconnect? Get curious about where the truth is. Be on the lookout for values that arise from things you "should" value such as societal norms, aspirational values, and inherited or imposed values that you may be trying to shake off.

4. Value visioning: Imagine yourself as the embodiment of your prioritized values. How does that person behave, interact, work, play, and rest? Do you like what you see?

5. Value legacy: Envision the personal and professional legacy you want to leave behind, and how living according to your values can help shape that legacy.

Mindfulness - Self-study at the Deepest Level

Let's talk about living a truly full life. To experience life to the fullest, we must be open to the entire range of human emotions. This is where many people get tripped up. They think being happy means only feeling positive emotions like joy and contentment. But they don't want to feel the tough ones—sadness, grief, anger, frustration. They even avoid so-called "neutral" emotions like boredom.

But to live wonderfully, we must embrace it all. We want to experience the highest highs, which requires being willing to go through the lowest lows too. To recognize the full emotional spectrum and not get stuck in the negative.

Saying "I never want to feel sad" is saying "I only want to be partially human," denying a piece of our humanity. And that's not compatible with a truly full life. We don't want to be half-in, we want to be all-in as fully devoted human beings.

Being willing to study yourself is an essential step on the path to leading a thriving life. Our minds are so tricky. We often can't discern what is real and what is our thought about what is happening. Of course, the starkest example of this would be to consider a patient with delirium or psychosis. They definitely can't discern their thoughts from reality and therefore their reality becomes a very scary place. But this happens to lesser degrees in human minds constantly.

The goal of mindfulness is to be able to step outside of this, to gain a little distance so that you can see what is going on from the outside. Think about how easy it is to see a situation clearly when a friend is telling you a story versus when you are living through it. Once we can get a little separation, we can start to see those patterns, the habits, the mind grooves that we have. By recognizing these, we can begin to figure out how to change. If we believe it is all real and true, then it is fixed. If we can step outside and see it as a set of patterns and habits, it is much easier to see how things can change. This is how we develop a growth mindset versus a fixed mindset.

We need to step outside ourselves and observe the feelings and thoughts we're having, recognizing they don't define us. It's like watching a movie of your own life, being able to see it a bit more objectively. Think about how much more clearly you can see a situation when a friend describes it, because you're outside of it. We want to cultivate that same outside perspective in our own lives.

The easiest initial step is a technique called noting. Noting means simply taking notice and labeling the present-moment experience as it arises, without judgment or analysis. "This feeling I'm experiencing is happiness…this is anger…this is boredom…" Or even more simply, "that is a thought…this is a feeling." Expanding our emotional vocabulary is step one. By developing the habit of noting and naming our internal experiences, we cultivate greater self-awareness and begin to distinguish the transient waves of thoughts and emotions from our enduring, grounded sense of self and values.

Noting allows us to see our mind's activity with a sense of curious detachment, recognizing that thoughts and feelings are temporary phenomena, not rigid definitions of who we are. As we label "this is anxiety," for instance, we create a subtle distance between our true self and the passing emotional state, preventing us from becoming entangled or overwhelmed by it. This practice of noting and naming lays the foundation for understanding our internal landscape with greater clarity and discernment.

Moreover, expanding our emotional vocabulary enriches our ability to navigate the nuances of our experiences with precision and depth. Instead of broadly categorizing emotions as "good" or "bad," we can develop a more refined emotional literacy, differentiating shades of joy, grief, longing, or contentment. This heightened awareness empowers us to respond to our emotions with wisdom and self-compassion, aligning our actions with our authentic values rather than reacting impulsively.

By cultivating the simple yet profound practice of noting and naming our present-moment experiences, we take the first step toward self-knowledge, emotional intelligence, and living a life grounded in our core values.

I teach my clients to practice the noting technique during regular seated meditation practice. Meditation is kind of like the mental gym where you get to practice all your techniques, you have them down pat when life demands use of them. Find guided meditations for noting and other mindfulness techniques on our website. Do you find yourself having resistance to practicing meditation or mindfulness? Here are a few reasons that might be happening and what you can do.

.Some people find the idea of sitting still and doing nothing a little intimidating, maybe even boring. Others might think they're too busy or that it's just some New Age fluff. But the heart of mindfulness is really about enhancing our connection to ourselves and our experiences. It's a valuable practice, no matter how busy we are or how daunting it might initially seem.

Start small. You don't have to spend an hour meditating. Just a few minutes focusing on your breath can work wonders. And it doesn't have to be formal meditation. You can practice mindfulness in everyday activities. Feel the warmth of the coffee mug in your hands, listen to the birds chirping outside, savor the flavor of your food. Remember, it's not about emptying your mind, it's about being present with what is. Like any skill, mindfulness takes practice. But with time and patience, it can become a natural part of your life.

Is that true? AKA don't believe everything you think.

This question has opened so many doors for me. It has also pulled the rug out from under me more than a few times. "Is that true" is a brave question that shows we are willing to examine our own assumptions.

Byron Katie is a renowned speaker and author who teaches a method of self-inquiry known as "The Work." The core of The Work involves questioning the thoughts that cause suffering through four simple yet powerful questions:

Is it true? (Yes or no)

Can you absolutely know that it's true?

How do you react when you believe that thought?

Who would you be without the thought?

By examining our thoughts through this line of questioning, we can identify which beliefs are actually true and which are perspectives or stories we've unconsciously bought into. This process helps break the spell that our thoughts can have over us.

Katie's approach also includes "turnarounds"—a way of experiencing the opposite of the original thought to allow space for other perspectives. The turnarounds reveal the reality that our thoughts are simply choices, not truth written in stone.

The ultimate goal of The Work is to achieve a state of personal freedom and peace by disidentifying from the thoughts that cause suffering and stress. When we realize our thoughts are not delivering an accurate picture of reality, we can let them go.

A key principle is to treat ourselves and others with radical self-honesty and compassion during this inquiry process. The Work is not about judging or berating ourselves, but meeting our thoughts and belief systems with courageous understanding.

With practice, people learn to experience their thoughts without attachment or aversion, opening to a spacious awareness beyond the conceptual mind. This liberates them to act from their deepest integrity and love rather than running on limiting mental projections.

Negative self-talk doesn't stand a chance once you hone your mindfulness skills. When those nasty little comments show up, you just say, "Oh hi, you little nasty comments you, I know you are just a thought and not the truth." Paired with self-compassion that everyone has thoughts like this, and you have just skated right by that moment of self-criticism without getting dragged down.

"I am failing at everything I do" – just a thought, no evidence to support.

"I am letting my kids down when I go to work" – hello THOUGHT, what else could be true?

"I am the dumbest doctor in this place" – technically this may be true for one person but it probably isn't you.

"I'm so stupid I can't even remember where I parked my car" – hi thought, may we have a little grace here, parking lots are large, and we have a lot on our minds.

"My kids will likely run away because I have deprived them of Pinterest-worthy lunchbox snacks" – hi thought, may I counter that your kids do not know what Pinterest is and definitely don't care.

"I ate a cookie and therefore have the worst nutrition of anyone who has ever lived, how can I possibly counsel patients now" – hi thought, may I offer you some great nutritional counseling about balance?

"My paper got rejected, I am a failure" – oh you sweet little thought, I know this one stings but it still ain't true.

"I feel sad and tired today, I am such a wreck of a person" – oh you sneaky little thought, you tried to come on in as an identity but I caught you. Not today!

Role of Therapy, Mentorship, and Coaching in Self-study

For many people, starting out on a journey of self-reflection can be intimidating. How do we know what questions to ask ourselves? What if something comes up that is just to big for us to hold alone? Once I identify some key areas for change, how do I know what to do? How do I go about shifting my mindset?

Therapy, mentorship, and coaching are all versions of support that can aide you on your self-study journey. Having another person holding space and providing insights and reflections is often incredibly valuable and will accelerate your progress. Many people benefit from a mix of all three. Here is how I make the distinction between these modalities so you can choose the one that seems like the right fit for you.

Therapy is a deep-dive into one's emotional state and past experiences, often guided by a trained professional. Therapists apply scientific methodologies to aid in understanding and navigating emotions, behaviors, and thoughts. This process is particularly beneficial for individuals grappling with life-altering experiences or mental health struggles. For instance, a healthcare professional dealing with the aftermath of a traumatic event may find therapy to be a valuable tool in her recovery process. Through therapy, she can address her fears, reduce anxiety, and learn coping mechanisms that promote healing and resilience.

Mentorship, on the other hand, is a relationship between an experienced individual (mentor) and someone less experienced (mentee), typically in a professional or academic setting. The mentor provides guidance, advice, and encouragement to the mentee. Mentorship may be particularly beneficial when considering your strengths and deciding how a specific career path aligns with your preferences. A seasoned mentor can share insights, provide support, and help the mentee hone her skills and expand her knowledge, empowering her to thrive in her chosen profession.

Coaching differs slightly from both therapy and mentorship. It is a process-oriented approach, typically focused on achieving specific personal or professional goals. The coach isn't necessarily an expert in the coachee's field but is equipped with the skills to facilitate the coachee's progress toward her objectives. A coach helps identify achievable goals, devise effective strategies, and maintain momentum even amid challenging circumstances.

As a coach, I hold my client's vision until they are strong enough to hold it themselves. My superpower is that I can see the future. I can see how wonderful things are going to be and how fulfilling and amazing life will be for you. I know that right now, you have a hood over your eyes. You are so clouded by overwhelm, burnout, exhaustion, self-doubt, insecurity, and shame that you can't see much of anything. So what I will do is tell you about it. I will describe the dream to give you hope. Then, together, we start to do things to remove the hood. Piece by piece, practice by practice, we get your sight back.

For many people, even once they can see clearly, the dream just feels too big. It seems impossible and this thought can send you back into the land of despair. As a coach, we continue to hold that dream with you until you trust you can hold it for yourself. As a coach I don't think I am saving you, because you don't need saving. You aren't broken. Coaching can be incredibly powerful and allow you to make progress faster and go farther than you ever could alone. But your coach can't just feed you a pill that magically makes everything different, you are the one who must do the work. This project is an inside job.

So yes, get as much help as you possibly can. Have a mentor *and* a coach *and* a therapist. Maybe even more than one of each. *And* commit to developing a habit of self-study.

Spheres of Control

The concept of "spheres of control" is rooted in Stoic philosophy, an ancient Greek school of thought that emphasized virtuous living and cultivating inner peace through rationality and self-control. In Stoicism, the idea of spheres of control relates to distinguishing between what is within our control and what is outside of our control. The Stoics believed that the only thing truly within our control is our own judgments, thoughts, and actions. External events, circumstances, and other people's behavior are outside of our direct control.

The Stoics taught that true happiness and tranquility come from focusing our efforts on what we can control (our responses) and not worrying about what we cannot control (external factors). By recognizing the limits of our influence, we can avoid frustration and anxiety over things beyond our power. In the twentieth century, Stephen Covey, the author of the influential book *The 7 Habits of Highly Effective People*, adapted and popularized this Stoic concept under the term "circles of concern and influence."

Covey's model includes three circles:

1. **Circle of Control**: This is the innermost circle, and it includes things you have direct control over. These might be your own behaviors, reactions, thoughts, feelings, and decisions. For instance, how you choose to react to criticism or your own work habits are within this circle.
2. **Circle of Influence**: This is the middle circle and contains things you can influence but not directly control. This might include the attitudes of your colleagues, how a group perceives you, or the

general morale of your team. You can sway or impact these things to some degree, but they're not completely within your control.
3. **Circle of Concern**: This is the outermost circle and includes things that concern you but are beyond your direct control or influence. This might include global events, the decisions of top executives in your company, or the overall direction of the economy.

Covey encouraged focusing energy and effort on the Circle of Influence, as this is where we can make the most positive impact. He advised against expending too much energy on the Circle of Concern, as this can lead to frustration, stress, and a sense of powerlessness.

By recognizing the spheres or circles within our control and directing our attention and efforts accordingly, we can cultivate a sense of personal responsibility, empowerment, and peace of mind, aligning with the core principles of Stoic philosophy.

Managing Burnout with the Spheres of Control Framework

1. **Focus on What You Can Control**: One key to managing burnout is to put most of your energy into things you can directly control. For example, if you're feeling overwhelmed by workload, you might not be able to control how much work is assigned to you, but you can control how you

prioritize tasks, how you manage your time, and when you take breaks.
2. **Influence Where You Can**: Use your energy in the Circle of Influence to build relationships, improve communication, and negotiate changes that can reduce stress and enhance productivity. For instance, if team dynamics are a source of stress, you might not be able to change every person's behavior, but through positive reinforcement, feedback, and modeling desired behaviors, you can influence the overall environment.
3. **Let Go of the Rest**: Recognize that there are things beyond both your control and influence. Spending too much emotional energy on these can be exhausting and can lead to burnout. Instead, try to acknowledge these concerns, but then shift your focus back to what you can control or influence.
4. **Self-Care**: Always remember that self-care is within your Circle of Control. You can decide to take breaks, engage in hobbies, meditate, exercise, and seek professional help if needed.

By understanding and applying the concept of spheres of control, individuals can better direct their energy toward productive actions, reduce feelings of helplessness or being overwhelmed, and build resilience against burnout.

Here are a few examples that come up frequently in the healthcare world.

Desired Outcome	Factors/Actions to Achieve the Outcome	Factors/Actions I Can Control	Factors/Actions Beyond My Control
I want my patients to be cured	- Administering the right treatment - Regular patient monitoring - Patient adherence to medication and advice	- Your own knowledge and skill in diagnosis and treatment - Frequency of monitoring and checkups you schedule for patients	- Patient's individual body response to treatment - Whether patients adhere to medication or advice outside the hospital/clinic
I want high patient satisfaction scores	- Clear communication - Timely treatment - Comfortable hospital environment	- Your bedside manner and communication style - Speed and efficiency of your provided care	- Hospital staffing and resource limitations - Potential administrative decisions that affect patient care - Patient's personal expectations or past experiences
I want a well-functioning team	- Regular team meetings - Open communication channels - Continuing education and training	- Your willingness to communicate openly - Taking initiatives for team meetings or training sessions - Being open to feedback	- Personalities and communication styles of colleagues - Administrative decisions on resource allocation for training - Hospital policies that might limit team initiatives

I want to be recognized for my important contribution to this organization	- High-quality patient care - Participation in committees or task forces - Sharing innovative ideas or best practices	- Consistently delivering quality care - Actively participating in meetings, committees, or projects - Proactively sharing knowledge, suggestions, or feedback with superiors	- Recognition practices of the organization - Perceptions or biases of superiors - Organizational politics or dynamics
Health insurance companies should make it easier for people to get the care they need	- Clear communication between providers and insurers - Simplified claim processes - Patient advocacy	- Ensuring all documentation and claims are correctly filled out and timely submitted - Educating patients about their insurance benefits - Building relationships with insurance representatives	- Insurance company policies and rules - National health policy regulations - Economic factors affecting insurance business models
Everyone should practice evidence-based medicine	- Continuing medical education - Access to current research and best practices - Collaboration and communication among healthcare professionals	- Actively seeking out and participating in continued education opportunities - Applying the latest evidence-based practices to your own work - Sharing new findings with colleagues and advocating for evidence-based practices in meetings	- Access to resources in some healthcare setting - Resistance to change among some professionals - Potential lack of updated resources or research on certain topics

We will revisit this concept in future chapters and consider the ways in which you can expand your circles of control and influence. By building strong communication skills and developing a network of advocacy, you can affect change and over time improve your circumstances. Now, however, the key self-study skill is to identify factors outside of your control and then do your best Elsa impression and LET IT GO!

Here are a few more examples we may encounter at home.

Desired Outcome	Factors/Actions to Achieve the Outcome	Factors/Actions I Can Control	Factors/Actions Beyond My Control
I want my spouse to help more with household chores	- Clear communication about needs - Setting a chore schedule - Positive reinforcement	- Expressing feelings and needs without blaming - Taking the initiative to create a shared chore list - Showing appreciation when the spouse helps	- Spouse's personal beliefs about roles in the household - Spouse's work schedule or stressors - Previous habits or upbringing of the spouse
I want my children to complete their homework	- Setting a consistent homework routine - Providing necessary resources (e.g., supplies, books) - Offering help or tutoring if needed	- Designating a specific homework time and space - Checking in on progress and offering assistance - Recognizing and rewarding consistent effort	- Children's individual learning styles or challenges - Quality of teaching or support they receive at school - Peer influences or distractions
I want everyone to clean up after themselves	- Setting clear house rules - Designating spaces for items	- Leading by example (putting things away after use)	- External schedules (e.g., kids' extracurriculars)

	- Regularly decluttering	- Organizing family tidying-up times - Offering incentives or rewards for maintaining tidiness	that might make routines challenging - Children's developmental stages and understanding of tidiness - Spouse's or children's inherent organizational habits
I want open communication within the family	- Regular family meetings or check-ins - Encouraging open dialogue - Ensuring a safe space for expression	- Initiating conversations about feelings or events - Actively listening without interruption or judgment - Sharing personal feelings and thoughts openly	- Innate personalities or communication styles of family members - External influences on family members (e.g., peer pressures on kids) - Past experiences or traumas that affect openness

Having fun identifying what is and is not within your control? You are going to love setting boundaries. Read on into the next chapter to learn more about how boundaries can increase your sphere of control and give you a better sense of order.

"When you say 'Yes' to others, make sure you are not saying 'No' to yourself."

– Paulo Coelho

CHAPTER 4
FORGING FIREPROOF BOUNDARIES:
PROTECTING YOUR WELL-BEING

We all know the story of three little pigs, right? Pig one built a house of straw, pig two built the house of twigs, and pig three built the house of bricks. And the big bad wolf comes by, and he huffs and puffs, and he blows down the straw and he blows down the twigs, but he doesn't blow down the bricks. Do you know why he couldn't blow down the bricks? Because the bricks were a firm boundary that was able to change the outcome. Straw and twigs were not firm enough boundaries to be able to change the outcome. The purpose of the boundary is not to change the external world, it changes your experience. We are not expecting the wolf not to huff and puff. He's a wolf. That's what he'll do. The purpose of the boundary is to keep piggy safe inside the house.

As you think about what kind of boundaries you need and why, be aware of the tendency to want to change external circumstances. It is one of the biggest mistakes we can make when we start to think about boundaries. We say, "I need a boundary," but what you're really saying is, "I want a way to control someone else's behavior." We don't have any way to control other people's behavior. We can train people how to interact with us through our boundaries. We can communicate clearly what is okay and what is not okay and give clear guidance on how to respect our boundaries. That we can do. But we cannot change other people's behavior.

So just like the big bad wolf was still going to huff and puff, he can learn that he can't blow down bricks, and he may eventually quit trying to blow down bricks. Maybe he'll go look for another house of twigs or maybe he will do some self-reflection and decide to collaborate with pigs instead of trying to destroy them. Whichever path the wolf chooses, it is his to choose and the only impact you have on it is by holding firm to your boundary. There is another way you can affect change, which is helping more piggies to build brick houses. If the wolf can't find any twig houses to blow down, he may be forced to change.

Boundaries, in essence, are the defining lines that mark off your emotional, physical, and psychological spaces. They indicate where one thing ends and another begins, where you end, and others begin. In the broadest sense, boundaries are about respect—self-respect, respect for others, and respect for the relationships we foster.

Think of boundaries like the banks of a river. The river flows best when it has well-defined banks to guide its course; otherwise, it spills over, causing destruction. Similarly, boundaries help channel our emotions, thoughts, and behaviors, keeping them within a healthy and constructive path. With well-defined boundaries, we avoid "flooding" ourselves and others, maintaining a balanced interaction and exchange.

One metaphor often used to describe boundaries is a property line around a house. Just as the property line delineates the physical area that your house occupies, your personal boundaries demarcate where you begin and end relative to others. Just as we wouldn't allow someone to randomly enter our house without permission, we shouldn't let others infringe on our emotional and psychological spaces without consent. Boundaries serve as the "fences" that ensure our personal "property" is respected.

In terms of personal relationships and interactions, consider boundaries as the rules in a game. Each game has a set of rules to ensure fair play, and without them, chaos ensues. Boundaries act as these rules in our interactions, ensuring each person is treated with respect, and preventing power imbalances or manipulation.

But why are boundaries important? First, they protect us. Like the protective shell of a turtle, they guard our personal space, our feelings, and our thoughts from potential harm. They help us preserve our physical, emotional, and mental well-being, preventing burnout, resentment, or violations of our rights.

Second, boundaries foster healthier relationships. When boundaries are clearly defined and respected, each party understands what is expected of them and how to treat one another. This mutual respect and understanding create an environment where trust and positive interactions can thrive.

Third, they promote personal growth and self-identity. Boundaries allow us to understand ourselves better, defining what we believe, what we value, and how we wish to be treated. They give us a clearer sense of self and help us stand up for our rights and needs.

Finally, boundaries support autonomy and self-esteem. As we learn to express and uphold our boundaries, we affirm that we are in charge of our lives and that our feelings, thoughts, and needs matter. This self-assertion can lead to greater self-confidence and self-respect.

Just as train tracks keep a train on course and prevent it from derailing, boundaries guide our interactions and prevent us from straying into potentially harmful territories. They are the essential "tracks" upon which our personal journeys run, crucial for a balanced, respected, and fulfilled existence.

When I was a young oncologist fresh out of fellowship, my views on boundaries and what it meant to be a good doctor were quite different than they are now. I believed that providing excellent care meant being the sole provider for my patients—their one and only. Continuity of care was paramount in my mind. Patients deserved to have someone consistently holding the thread of their care who they knew and trusted.

While I still value continuity, I no longer believe one person should shoulder that responsibility alone 24/7/365. But back then, that's exactly how I structured my practice for patients on my panel who had cancer or serious blood conditions—many of them children and their families. I made it clear they would always see me, no matter what.

If I was on hospital service or had administrative days, I would still come in to see patients who needed visits. After-hours or on weekends, rather than having the on-call provider field calls, I took them directly. If a patient had an issue while I was on vacation, I expected nurses and the covering doctor to call me so I could be involved. I routinely gave patients my cell number to call me, bypassing the typical channels.

I didn't take much time off in those days. It was a busy life stage with two young kids at home. We were also paying off loans, so vacation travel wasn't in our budget. But we did take the kids to Disney World one year. While there, one of my patients became critically ill and ultimately passed away that week.

Because of how I had set things up, the hospital team ended up calling me constantly with updates from across the country. I was desperately trying to remotely manage this patient's care from an amusement park—a losing battle that only distracted me from my family's vacation. In hindsight, although I was this child's doctor who knew them well, not being there in person severely limited my ability to effectively direct their care during such an acute crisis.

I even recall weighing whether to cut our trip short and fly home, which seems ludicrous given the expense and my kids' excitement about Disney. But that's how invested I had become in this dysfunctional dynamic where I believed quality care could only come from me personally. If I wasn't available, it inherently meant substandard care in my mind.

Looking back, that mentality was not only detrimental to my own wellbeing but also did a disservice to patients. By setting myself up as the sole provider of proper care, I was signaling that other doctors on my team were unqualified—that patients shouldn't fully trust them because they didn't manage things exactly like me. So anytime I was unavailable, whether on vacation or simply getting sick myself, patients felt they were receiving inferior care.

The truth is, no individual, no matter their efforts or sacrifices, can be available 24/7/365. We are human with our own needs and personal lives. Emergencies, illnesses, and obligations will inevitably take us away at times. By creating a cult of myself as the only good doctor, I disrespected my colleagues' abilities and led patients to feel abandoned whenever I was physically or mentally unable to provide coverage.

Now, I believe the best approach is recognizing that quality care stems from a well-designed care team and system—not any single provider's heroic efforts. My personal excellence matters, but just as importantly, our practice needs robust systems in place to ensure patients always feel supported and receive appropriate care access, regardless of my individual availability.

Upholding sustainable boundaries around things like schedules, call coverage, and division of responsibilities is critical for preventing burnout and providing high-quality patient care long-term. When I violated boundaries by trying to be available at all times, it ultimately undermined the system's ability to function effectively for my patients.

For example, if I made exceptions for complicated cases by telling the residents to call me rather than the appropriate covering doctor, it sent the message that our call system was inadequate for complex patients. It planted doubts that any doctor besides me could properly manage their care. Residents then started viewing me as the only safe option for sick patients on weekends or nights.

This not only contradicted our protocols, but more concerningly, it perpetuated the unhealthy belief that quality care hinged on me alone rather than our collective healthcare team and processes. If a resident felt they couldn't fully trust the on-call attending with a critically ill patient because "that's Dr. Jones' patient," it subverted our entire system's credibility.

Likewise, when I stepped outside boundaries to take calls while on vacation or inserted myself into care remotely from afar, it likely made patients question whether our coverage plans were sufficient. Why would their doctor need to get involved if we had a reliable system for when she's unavailable? It planted seeds of doubt.

The more I made individual exceptions as a workaround, rather than identifying and addressing system limitations, the more I undermined our protocols' integrity in both my colleagues' and patients' eyes. I was effectively communicating that our processes couldn't be trusted for delivering consistent, high-quality care.

What I've realized is that sometimes we have to bravely let small failures or imperfect situations play out in order to reveal the need for larger system changes. While difficult, it's better than perpetually individually overriding the system with cumbersome workarounds. Those Band-Aids breed distrust in our processes and keep us from enacting meaningful improvements. And they expect superhuman acts of "going above and beyond" which are ultimately destructive to our own well-being.

For example, if our call system failed one weekend and a patient couldn't reach the covering doctor, the answer should not be to give every patient my cell number. We should address this issue as a system, document the failure, and conduct a root cause analysis which allows for a rational solution to the actual problem. Maybe we need to advocate for stronger backup call processes going forward, or maybe our communications carrier is unreliable. The truth is, this may not be a one-off issue and by failing to address it at a systems level, we may be postponing awareness of a problem that affects multiple departments and thousands of patients. As clinicians, we must resist the urge to put out every fire ourselves and strive to make our systems better.

Clear communication with patients about care team roles, availability expectations, and contingency plans is also crucial. We may assume they understand concepts like "on-call," but many don't. By explicitly explaining who will be involved in their care, what qualifications they have, why we follow certain protocols, and what to expect in terms of responsiveness, we increase transparency and buy-in.

Ultimately, we want patients to trust our practice's full system and team for delivering consistent, quality care—not just place blind faith in one individual provider. Sustainable boundaries and protocols that respect the humanity of all staff, paired with open communication, allow us to share that load and set families at ease. While my passion for going the extra mile came from a good place initially, not setting boundaries ultimately eroded our ability to provide the excellent care I aspired to in the first place.

Discussion of boundaries is integral to discussion of burnout recovery and prevention. So many of the wounds we sustain could be prevented if we had a proper boundary in place. Boundaries are also how we participate in systems change. If we want the system to move toward one that recognizes the humanity of healthcare workers, our need for rest, our emotional burdens, etc., we must first recognize them in ourselves and set up personal systems to enforce them. If everyone suddenly quit going "above and beyond" or being a healthcare hero, the deficiencies in the system would rapidly become apparent and the pressures to resolve them much greater on the higher-ups and key decision-makers.

Key mindset shifts:

- Boundaries are good and necessary for our own well-being.
- Boundaries are an essential ingredient in social and systems change.

Why these shifts? The baseline mindset of most people in healthcare is that the patient comes first. Self-sacrifice is applauded and rewarded and setting boundaries about our time is seen as selfish and "not being a good team player." We are also in the habit of considering the person directly in front of us more importantly than the system at large. And we are good people, we don't want to see something fall through the cracks because we are upholding a boundary.

Physical Boundaries

Physical boundaries are among the easiest ones to understand. This is the type of boundary we exercise when we say what is and is not okay with our physical space and touching. Asking someone to step back a bit or refrain from hugging are very clear forms of physical boundaries. Setting limits with our time is also a form of physical boundary and one that can be a great place to start practicing boundary-setting.

Physical boundaries pertain to personal space and physical touch. They are the easiest to identify because they're tangible. Examples include not touching people without their permission, respecting others' personal space, or knocking before entering a patient's room.

Emotional Boundaries

Emotional boundaries are how we protect our hearts from being swallowed up by the emotional experience of others. Say you are in a patient encounter and have just told someone some very difficult news. They are likely to have a strong emotional reaction, possibly sadness expressed by crying or anguished sobs, or anger, or even confusion or disbelief. Having an emotional boundary means that you very clearly see the difference between their pain and your pain. You don't empathize with them so much that you also *feel* the way they feel.

This type of boundary is also essential with our colleagues. Say your coworker has just had a very frustrating encounter with an insurance company and the treatment she was advocating for has been denied. She comes to your office door mad as a wet hen and ready to vent. Having an emotional boundary that you will not take on her frustration and will remain separated from the situation will allow you to give her a little space to vent without it ruining your whole day too. By the way, a physical boundary can also be helpful in this situation by setting a time limit on the venting. This is beneficial for both you and her. Endless venting does not solve anything, and it doesn't actually make us feel better.

Emotional boundaries involve separating your feelings from another's feelings. They are violated when someone criticizes, belittles, or invalidates another person's feelings. A healthcare provider should maintain emotional boundaries by not taking on the patient's emotional burdens as their own, and not sharing their personal problems with the patient.

Emotional boundaries are important in healthcare settings to ensure the emotional well-being of both the healthcare providers and patients. These boundaries separate an individual's feelings from another's and protect emotional energy. Here are ten examples of emotional boundaries in a healthcare setting:

1. Separating Feelings: Healthcare providers should keep their emotions separate from their patients', preventing themselves from taking on the emotional burden of their patients.

2. Patient's Emotional Burdens: Healthcare providers should not make the patient's emotional burdens their own. Empathize with the patient, but also recognize the importance of detaching oneself from their emotional struggles.

3. Sharing Personal Life: A healthcare provider should not share personal life details or emotional issues with the patient, even if the patient asks. This can blur the lines of the professional relationship.

4. Patient's Emotions: While it's important to validate the patient's feelings and emotions, it's equally important not to let those emotions dictate the healthcare provider's actions or treatment decisions.

5. Coping Mechanisms: Providers should not impose their own coping mechanisms on the patient (or colleague), but rather help them develop their own strategies to deal with their emotions.

6. Personal Reactions: Healthcare providers should avoid reacting to a patient's emotional outburst personally.

7. Uncomfortable Topics: Providers should not press patients to discuss emotionally charged topics if they are not comfortable doing so.

8. Emotional Investment: Healthcare providers should avoid becoming overly emotionally invested in the outcome of a patient's treatment. It's important to care, but this should not lead to distress if a patient doesn't follow advice or their condition worsens.

9. Overstepping Emotional Limits: Providers should not allow patients to overstep their emotional limits, like seeking emotional support or treating them as a friend or family member.

10. Subjectivity and Bias: Providers should not let their own feelings about a certain patient or situation affect their professional judgment or the quality of care provided.

Here's a hypothetical situation that demonstrates a violation of emotional boundaries:

Dr. Jane is a well-regarded general practitioner who has a patient, Mr. Smith, suffering from chronic depression. Mr. Smith has been her patient for several years now, and over time, Dr. Jane has grown particularly fond of him due to his kind demeanor and appreciation for her help.

One day, Mr. Smith comes in for a routine visit, visibly upset. He shares with Dr. Jane that his wife recently left him, and he's been having suicidal thoughts. Dr. Jane, already emotionally attached to Mr. Smith, immediately feels a rush of sadness and anxiety on hearing this news. She begins to share with him her own experience of going through a divorce, her ensuing depression, and how she managed to cope. She even starts crying during the conversation, saying how hard it was for her and that she understands exactly what he's going through.

In an attempt to support Mr. Smith, Dr. Jane gives him her personal phone number and urges him to call her anytime he feels the need, even in the middle of the night. She also offers to introduce him to her brother who is a life coach, hoping this might help him get through his crisis.

While Dr. Jane's intentions may have been good, her actions breach several emotional boundaries. Sharing personal experiences to this extent and becoming emotionally affected during a patient consultation is unprofessional. It can blur the line between the professional and personal relationship, making it confusing for the patient. Moreover, providing personal contact details for out-of-hours emotional support is inappropriate, potentially leading to boundary confusion and overdependence on Dr. Jane. Finally, suggesting her brother's help could also be perceived as a conflict of interest and does not uphold the objectivity that should be present in a professional healthcare setting.

Psychological Boundaries

Psychological boundaries are a bit more complex, as they pertain to a person's thoughts, values, and beliefs. These are violated when someone tries to manipulate or control another person's thoughts or impose their beliefs onto others. Examples of maintaining psychological boundaries in a healthcare setting would include respecting a patient's autonomy, not imposing personal beliefs or decisions on the patient, and not providing advice outside your area of expertise.

1. Professional Relationships: A healthcare professional should not form intimate relationships with their patients. This boundary is necessary to prevent undue influence or manipulation of thoughts and emotions.

2. Self-Disclosure: A healthcare provider should limit self-disclosure to situations that benefit the therapeutic process. Oversharing can blur the professional boundary and may inadvertently shift focus onto the healthcare provider's issues.

3. Dual Relationships: Avoiding relationships with patients outside of the healthcare context. This boundary prevents potential conflicts of interest and manipulative dynamics.

4. Respect for Autonomy: Respect for patient autonomy and not imposing personal beliefs or decisions on them. This is crucial for respecting the patient's individual identity, beliefs, and agency.

5. Therapeutic Decisions: Decisions about treatment should always be in the best interest of the patient, not based on personal gain or convenience. This ensures the patient's thoughts and desires are prioritized.

6. Personal Information: Avoid asking patients for information that's not relevant to their healthcare. This

can help to avoid invading their privacy or manipulating them.

7. Respect for Cultural Differences: Respect for a patient's cultural or religious practices and not imposing your own. This is vital to respect the patient's personal beliefs and values.

8. Professional Advice: Do not provide advice outside your area of expertise. This boundary prevents potential manipulation or imposition of personal beliefs.

9. Patient Dependency: Avoid creating a situation where the patient becomes excessively dependent on the healthcare provider. This can prevent undue influence and manipulation of the patient's thoughts and decisions.

Here's another hypothetical scenario:

Nurse Alice has been working in the pediatric ward for several years and has formed strong emotional bonds with many of her young patients. She cares deeply for their well-being, often going beyond her role to comfort them and their worried parents.

One day, she meets a young girl named Lucy, who has been diagnosed with a severe form of leukemia. Alice quickly forms a bond with Lucy due to her radiant smile and positive attitude, reminding her of her own daughter at home.

Lucy's treatment proves to be particularly challenging, resulting in prolonged stays at the hospital. As the days turn into weeks, Alice starts spending her lunch breaks, free time, and sometimes even after-hours with Lucy, reading her stories, playing games, and trying to keep her spirits up.

Soon, Alice starts to share details about her own life, her family, and how she worries about her daughter every day. She tells Lucy how seeing her so brave gives her strength. She also shares her worries about Lucy's condition, often tearing up in front of her and her family. She even discusses Lucy's case with her own family at home, becoming more and more emotionally invested in the outcomes of Lucy's treatment.

Despite Alice's good intentions, her actions display a clear breach of emotional boundaries. She has allowed her personal feelings to become entwined with her professional responsibilities, leading to an overly personal relationship with her patient. By sharing her fears and worries, she's potentially adding to the emotional burden of Lucy and her family, rather than lessening it. Discussing Lucy's case with her family at home also violates confidentiality norms. This level of emotional involvement may not only affect Alice's professional judgment but also her own emotional well-being and the quality of care she provides to her other patients.

I hope you can see from these examples this importance of holding boundaries. Although it may feel difficult initially, it leads to more ease and authentic connection down the line. Mindfulness skills are very important in discerning emotions from facts and help you keep a level head as you are making treatment plans. One key mantra to remember when holding boundaries is "you are not me." This helps us to remember that what may be very helpful to us or make perfect sense to us, may not be to the other person. They have a completely different set of experiences, values, strengths, and circumstances. It's not about you.

See the problem to be addressed as separate from both you and the patient. You are working together to address the problem; this will help prevent you from taking things personally. A small amount of self-disclosure can help build rapport but keep it light. "I love pasta too" is safe. "My mother also has cancer and I'm going to tell you all about it," is crossing a boundary.

In the next chapter, I will teach you the keys to having difficult conversations with ease. Remembering to respect the patient's boundaries within such conversations is also important. Your comfort level with a topic is likely very different from the patient's. Ask for an invitation to discuss topics that may be difficult. "Would it be okay if I told you more about what to expect during the surgery?" Or "May I ask you more about how you are coping with this new diagnosis?" We don't have a right to their sensitive information. It is our duty to skillfully build rapport and create a container in which people feel comfortable sharing. Respect their boundaries of choosing what they do and do not want to talk about with you.

The Need to be Liked: Exploring the Psychological Underpinnings

At the core of many boundary violations in healthcare lies a fundamental human need—the need to be liked and accepted. This desire for validation and approval is deeply rooted in our psychological makeup, stemming from an evolutionary drive to belong to a group and ensure our survival.

The Role of Validation and Self-Worth

For many healthcare professionals, their sense of self-worth is closely tied to their work and the perception others have of them. The need for validation from patients, colleagues, and superiors can be overwhelming, as it provides a sense of purpose and reassurance that they are valued and appreciated. However, when this need for validation becomes excessive, it can lead to compromising one's boundaries in an attempt to please others and gain their approval.

The Desire for Approval and Acceptance

Closely linked to the need for validation is the desire for approval and acceptance. Healthcare professionals often find themselves in situations where they are expected to go above and beyond, sacrificing their personal time and well-being to meet the demands of their patients or colleagues. The fear of being perceived as uncaring or unprofessional can drive individuals to disregard their own boundaries, leading to burnout and emotional exhaustion.

The Impact of Societal and Cultural Expectations

Societal and cultural expectations also play a significant role in shaping the need to be liked in healthcare settings. The perception of healthcare professionals as selfless caregivers who put the needs of others before their own can create immense pressure to conform to these idealized standards. This can lead to a reluctance to set boundaries, as it may be perceived as a sign of weakness or a lack of dedication to one's profession.

Strategies for Addressing the Need for Validation in a Healthy Manner

My own experiences as a young oncologist fresh out of fellowship illustrate how the need for validation and the desire to be perceived as a dedicated, selfless provider can lead to unhealthy boundary violations.

In hindsight, I recognize that my actions stemmed from a belief that providing excellent care meant being the sole provider for my patients—their one and only source of support. There was an underlying need for my patients' unwavering approval and trust, which led me to disregard personal boundaries and sacrifice my own well-being. The fear of being perceived as anything less than a committed, selfless caregiver drove me to overextend myself, ultimately compromising the quality of care I could provide in the long run.

This personal experience highlights the importance of developing self-awareness and finding a balance between meeting the needs of patients and maintaining one's own emotional and physical boundaries. While the desire for validation is natural, it should not come at the expense of our own well-being or the integrity of the healthcare system. We must find healthy ways to address these needs without compromising one's boundaries.

Some strategies that may help include:

- Cultivating self-awareness and self-acceptance: Recognizing and acknowledging your own inherent worth and value, independent of external validation.
- Building a strong support system: Surrounding yourself with individuals who offer genuine support and encouragement, without the need for constant approval.
- Seeking professional guidance: Working with a therapist or coach to explore the underlying reasons for the need for validation and developing healthy coping mechanisms.
- Practicing self-care: Engaging in activities that promote self-nurturing and personal growth, reinforcing the importance of prioritizing your own well-being.
- Reframing perspectives: Challenging societal and cultural expectations that perpetuate the need for constant approval and instead embracing a more balanced and realistic view of one's role as a healthcare professional.

In most cases when I see people living with poor boundaries, the need to be liked is lurking in there somewhere. I do want to distinguish this from the need for love, respect, dignity, or compassion. Everyone deserves love and respect, and in the following chapters we are going to discuss communication techniques and community-building strategies so that you get the things you need to truly fill up your cup.

Anyone who has parented a teenager knows that even though you love them, you may not always like what they are doing. Similarly, most of us would easily reject the idea that our value is dependent on the number of "likes" we get on a social media post. We want to develop innate confidence and a small circle of trusted advisors, so that we no longer run our lives by public opinion poll. How do you think Alice Waters would respond if she prepared a delicious farm-to-table meal with fresh seasonal ingredients and then served it to a three-year-old who said, "I don't like it" because they prefer mac and cheese. I am quite sure her belief in her cooking talents would not be shaken.

Here's another example of how our ego attachments and desire for validation can get us into trouble.

I work with a neonatologist who is part of a group practice that serves several area hospitals. At our first meeting, she told me about a mess that was causing her a lot of angst and keeping her up at night. She had recently missed a phone call from a parent which led to them feeling abandoned and unsure that their child was getting the best care. She was wracked with guilt. She had turned her phone off for the afternoon while out on a hike with her family and returned home to frantic voicemails and texts, which ruined her night and most of the next day.

Let's take a look backward and see how some boundary setting might have helped here.

The practice operates on a rotating schedule, with doctors frequently moving between different hospital sites every week. Many families expressed difficulty bonding with a new doctor each week, prompting Dr. X and her colleagues to provide their cell phone numbers in order to be "good doctors."

While this practice initially made Dr. X feel appreciated and validated that she was a dedicated physician, it quickly spiraled into an unsustainable situation. Families would frequently call multiple neonatologists, even those not currently assigned to their case, seeking second opinions or conflicting advice. This undermined the care plan established by the on-site physician and potentially introduced biases, as doctors may have subconsciously prioritized responding to certain patients over others, seeking that dopamine hit of validation and ego-stroking.

Of course, this approach also intruded into their personal lives. Dr X shared with me one instance in which she was at her son's basketball game. He was glancing over at her every few seconds to make sure she was watching. But she has to take the call, these babies are fighting for their lives. The people-pleasing martyr complex was in full swing. The psychological toll of never truly being "off the clock" was immense, denying her the rest and respite necessary for her own well-being.

Perhaps most concerningly, this practice set up unrealistic expectations for the patients. By conditioning families to rely solely on the validation and reassurance of specific neonatologists like Dr. X, it created a situation where any unavailability on her part, whether due to illness, personal obligations, or rotating assignments, was perceived as abandonment. Families might feel unable to trust the care decisions of the on-site physician, palliative care team, or other healthcare professionals they had known for months, simply because their trusted neonatologist was not present.

The road to hell is paved with good intentions. Without clear boundaries and rigorous practices to set and enforce them, we can easily get ourselves into trouble. This case study illustrates how the need for validation and the desire to be perceived as a dedicated, selfless provider can drive healthcare professionals like Dr. X to overstep boundaries in ways that ultimately undermine the quality of care and negatively impact both the providers and the patients themselves.

Now I am not saying we should aim to make people unhappy. Just recognize that people's initial happy/unhappy reaction may not be in tune with what is actually good for the situation. Develop a practice of curiosity and humility. Imagine in the scenario above, the doctors had stayed curious and asked the question "how can we improve continuity from week to week and ensure patients feel supported" while staying humble and open to solutions that involved team members and didn't focus on their ego or reputation. Likely this would involve solutions that leverage the nurses or other team members who don't rotate sites or could involve a warm handoff between doctors that includes the patients. I'm not an expert in NICU operations, so I won't speculate further. The point is, including boundaries and physician sustainability is an important part of considering solutions.

And boundaries must be rules because it is so easy to slip under or around them. This can sometimes make it feel rigid or unnuanced. In my youth, I also rejected such ideas of boundaries and wanted to be able to take a case-by-case basis.

There is truth in the understanding of a boundary as it isn't what you do, it's why you do it. For example, attending a patient's birthday party or funeral. These activities can be lovely expressions of our shared humanity and a way to develop a deeper understanding of the patients you care for. But these can easily slip into ego-driven activities in which we show up to get brownie points as a caring physician or bask in the accolades from the friends and family. So unless you can ensure you have some pretty tight self-examination practices, it may be best to just have a rule that you don't do personal events like this.

Same goes for social media engagement (for your personal accounts)—it's probably best to have a strict role that you don't engage with patients there.

So how do we have deep, human connection with our patients and colleagues while maintaining great boundaries? Here's an example of how this can be done:

Dr. Carter has been treating Mr. Thompson for an aggressive form of cancer for several years. Unfortunately, despite their best efforts, all treatment options have been exhausted and Mr. Thompson's health continues to decline.

As she prepares to meet with Mr. Thompson and his family, Dr. Carter carefully considers her words. It's important to her that she conveys her concern and deep sadness about the situation, but she also recognizes the importance of maintaining her professional role as his doctor.

She starts the conversation by acknowledging the journey they've taken together and expressing gratitude for the trust Mr. Thompson and his family have placed in her over the years.

"Mr. Thompson, we've been on a long journey together. I want to acknowledge your strength and resilience throughout this entire process, and I want to thank you for the trust you've placed in me as your doctor."

Next, she delivers the difficult news with honesty and sensitivity, making sure to focus on Mr. Thompson's feelings and reactions.

"I want to discuss the current situation honestly. Despite our best efforts and exhausting all available treatment options, your condition is unfortunately continuing to worsen. This deeply saddens me. We have been through a lot together and I truly wish we could have achieved a better outcome."

She then takes the time to listen to Mr. Thompson and his family, providing space for their reactions and emotions. She shows her empathy and understanding, without sharing her personal feelings.

"I understand that this is difficult news. It's okay to have strong emotions, and I'm here to provide support in any way I can. Do you have any questions or concerns you would like to discuss?"

Throughout the conversation, Dr. Carter expresses her care and concern, while also maintaining her professional role as Mr. Thompson's physician. By focusing on Mr. Thompson's feelings rather than her own, she maintains appropriate emotional boundaries, even in the face of a deeply upsetting situation.

Boundaries Give You More Flexibility, Not Less

Your no's protect your yes's. If you get in a habit of saying yes to everything out of people pleasing or chasing business, or whatever reason, you really are just saying you are giving up control of what you actually say yes to. No human can actually do everything. So by not being intentional with your time and saying yes only to those things you care about and want to devote time and energy to, you set up a free-for-all in which the squeakiest wheel will get your attention and some things will just haphazardly fall to the wayside.

We may feel that not having "rigid" rules allows us to be free. But this is often the opposite. Have you ever had a day in which you had nothing scheduled? Maybe you had some ideas of what you would like to do that day but somehow the calendar was empty. For me, these days are the worst. I often spend hours just trying to figure out what I want to do and then beat myself up because I didn't do anything. I didn't schedule anything because "I don't want to be tied down" and wanted to be able to follow my mood. Now I use a strategy of scheduling some anchors throughout the day. A walk to the coffee shop, a yoga class at the studio, or a scheduled time to go to the grocery store. Having these anchors opens the day.

Similarly, having a few rules about my nutrition helps me immensely. I eat fruit for breakfast, avoid sugar during the workday, and have a meal on a plate at dinnertime. Around that I can do whatever I want. These few "rigid rules" make sure I keep mostly on track with my goals and make it easier to make the choices that come up—like what to eat for lunch or afternoon snack. Another way I have used "rules" to help me with nutrition was having a weekly roadmap of dinner plans. Monday beans, Tuesday fish, Wednesday grain bowl, Thursday sandwich, etc. This structure narrowed down the breadth of possibilities for each day and made decision-making about what to eat much easier. It also set clear expectations for my family and reduced anxiety about what was for dinner.

See, boundaries can be your friend. Embrace the boundary lifestyle. Become a boundary evangelist for your friends and family. It will change your life.

Establishing boundaries does not mean being inflexible or rigid. It's about creating a space that safeguards your emotional, physical, and psychological well-being while also respecting others'. Here are a few strategies to help maintain boundaries without becoming overly rigid:

- Balance: Remember that boundaries are not about isolation but about balance. Effective boundaries allow for connection and interaction, but in a manner that respects individual autonomy and comfort levels.
- Flexibility: Adapt your boundaries according to different situations or relationships. A boundary with a close friend may differ from that with a work colleague. Understand that boundaries can be flexible and adapt as circumstances and relationships evolve.
- Clear Communication: Clearly communicate your boundaries to others but be open to discussion. It's important to be firm yet kind in expressing your limits, but also willing to listen to the other person's perspective. More on communication in chapter 5!

- **Understanding Others' Boundaries:** Just as you have your own boundaries, others have theirs too. Respect them and learn to work within those limits. Understanding and empathy should be reciprocal.
- **Regular Reviews:** Regularly revisit your boundaries. As you grow and evolve, so may your boundaries. Periodically reassess whether your boundaries are still serving you or if they need adjustment.
- **Negotiation and Compromise:** Sometimes you may need to negotiate boundaries with others or even make certain compromises, particularly in relationships where there's a significant level of trust and understanding. Communication skills are important here too.

Remember, boundaries are not walls but guidelines. They are not meant to be unyieldingly rigid or isolating, but to facilitate healthier interactions, greater self-respect, and overall well-being. The key is to find that fine line between safeguarding your personal space and maintaining meaningful connections with others.

Setting Boundaries to Protect Your Peace

Using boundaries to protect your peace means putting limits around your time, energy, and attention. The two key skills are learning to say no gracefully and practicing focused attention. Without boundaries, people will continue to expect you to sacrifice your own well-being for their demands.

Most of us have already established patterns and expectations with the people in our lives. They may expect us to do things outside our roles or responsibilities simply because we've never declined before. To reset these dynamics, we need to start saying no kindly yet firmly to reprogram expectations around us.

For example, consider Dr. C, a hospitalist I worked with in a busy group practice. She was feeling overwhelmed by constantly working extra shifts to be a "good teammate." Through self-reflection, she identified that working more than one night shift per week left her completely drained, impacting her health. She implemented a firm boundary—if she already had one night shift scheduled and another was requested, she would decline.

Importantly, Dr. C also realized that some extra work did align with her values, as it provided income to pay for her children's college. So when a shift didn't violate her one night per week limit, she could say yes without feeling overwhelmed. Her mantra became "I'm helping as much as I can while preserving my well-being."

Dr. C's experience highlights how clear boundaries can protect you from overcommitting while still allowing you to wholeheartedly engage in opportunities that genuinely enrich your life. Defined limits make you more intentional about where you expend your finite time and energy.

In addition to boundaries around your time commitments, it's crucial to set boundaries around your attention. In the previous chapter on self-study, we explored mindfulness practices for focusing your attention. Without intentional boundaries, distractions and demands on your attention can deplete your energy and presence.

Maintaining boundaries around your attention allows you to be fully engaged with your current task or interaction. When you're with your family, are you truly present or constantly pulled away by pings and notifications? When you're at work, are you able to concentrate deeply or continually context-switching between competing demands?

Establishing habits like disabling notifications, scheduling tech-breaks, practicing meditation, and *single tasking* can help fortify your attentional boundaries. You're in control of where you direct your focused awareness. Protecting that stream of attention from constant dispersal is key to feeling grounded and replenishing your energetic reserves.

Dr. C's mantra of "helping as much as I can while preserving my well-being" encompasses guarding both her time and attentional boundaries. She created space to be fully present for patient interactions, her own self-care practices, and quality time with loved ones—instead of being perpetually fragmented. Mindfully choosing where to direct your attention fortifies your boundaries and sense of inner peace.

It's Hard at First, Embrace the Journey

This is a poem called "Autobiography in Five Short Chapters" by Portia Nelson. I love this story for understanding the nonlinear nature of progress. I also love this story because it gives me a visual to understand the landscape of the work I need to do and the boundaries that may be beneficial.

Chapter 1
I walked down the street.
There is a deep hole in the sidewalk.
I fall in.
I am lost. I am helpless.
It isn't my fault.
It still takes forever to find a way out.

Chapter 2
I walked down the same street.
There is a deep hole in the sidewalk.
I pretend I don't see it.
I fall in again.
I can't believe I'm in the same place.
But it isn't my fault.
It still takes a long time to get out.

Chapter 3
I walk down the same street.
There is a deep hole in the sidewalk.
I see it is there.

> I still fall in… It's a habit…but my eyes are open.
> I know where I am.
> It is my fault.
> I get out immediately.
>
> Chapter 4
> I walk down the same street
> There is a deep hole in the sidewalk.
> I walk around it.
>
> Chapter 5
> I walk down a different street.

Alright, read it again.

Let's just take a few breaths to think about which chapter resonates with you the most right now.

Do you feel like you are still just walking down the same street and falling in the same hole? Maybe you're stuck on chapter one. Like you can't even see the hole you haven't figured out, you just keep making the same mistakes and having the same problems but can't even see them. Or maybe you're in chapter two, where you know that it's there, but your mind is still fluctuating so much and telling you a story and making you think that it's not there. So when this first says I pretend I don't see it, it may be my mind's telling me a story that it's not there. Or maybe you're in chapter three, where you see it and you still fall in because again, you've still got that story that you need that hole for some reason. Like that hole is part of who you are. So that may be where you are, in chapter three. And that's where I was the first time I heard this. I felt really called out by this, I may have even spoken to it with something like, "You don't know me, how dare you tell me something about myself!"

Because I knew that I was going into the same patterns over and over and over again. But it was a habit. And I was somewhere between denying it and recognizing that it's my fault. I think that was the part that I felt really called out by like, oh yeah, keep jumping in the same hole. Maybe that's my fault. So maybe you're on chapter three like I was. Maybe you're on chapter four, which is great. You're making progress. You've identified the hole and you're taking action. And maybe you're in chapter five, you've actually changed the story and walked down a different street and made lots of good choices.

You may notice that you are on a different journey for various domains of your life. Maybe there's a relationship story that you're on one chapter and a work story that you're on a different chapter and maybe a personal habit like exercise or dealing with alcohol that you're on a different story, a different chapter in your story.

Is there a hole in the street that you keep falling in? Why do you keep going down the same street if there's a hole? That's not the way you set a boundary, the way you set a boundary is by walking down a different street.

As we wrap up this chapter on boundaries, reflect on the clear need for effective communication to support your ability to establish and uphold your boundaries. I use this quote by Brené Brown as a mantra to guide my words: *Clear is Kind, Unclear is Unkind.*

Here are a few more specific tips on communicating boundaries:

- Embrace the principle that "clear is kind, unclear is unkind"—direct, assertive communication prevents misunderstandings and upholds boundaries.
- Develop assertiveness skills like saying "no" firmly but emphatically, using "I" statements, and avoiding apologetic language when setting limits.
- Manage unrealistic demands by compassionately identifying unreasonable requests, providing explanations, and offering alternative solutions.
- Establish clear professional boundaries by defining appropriate provider-patient relationships, explaining limits on personal disclosures, and discussing policies around after-hours communication.
- Foster a culture of mutual understanding by collaborating with colleagues, aligning on shared boundaries/expectations, and addressing violations professionally.
- Prioritize continuing education on communication skills, role-playing exercises, and seeking feedback to reinforce boundary-setting abilities.

Knowing that you can find the words to convey your boundary and trusting that you can navigate a difficult conversation when it arises are essential phoenix skills. In the next chapter we will learn practical techniques to face even the toughest blaze of conversation. We will also put our self-study and boundary-setting skills to the test and consider those times when it is best to say nothing at all.

"Daring to set boundaries is about having the courage to love ourselves, even when we risk disappointing others."

- Brené Brown,
The Gifts of Imperfection

CHAPTER 5
COMMUNICATING THROUGH THE SMOKE:
CLEAR MESSAGES FOR A CLEARER PATH

So far we have learned about the importance of rest and our right to claim space for ourselves in our lives. We have learned to look inward and find out who we truly are and how to use boundaries to protect our peace. Up to this point, most of the work is internal. You may have successfully made some of the huge mindset shifts in the prior chapters without having to tell anyone else about it.

Now it is time to take this outside ourselves. In this chapter, we are going to learn how to tell others about our needs so that we can develop and deepen the human connections necessary for flourishing.

Imagine yourself in a bustling kitchen, apron on, skillet in hand, flames flickering, and ingredients sizzling. The room is filled with the clatter of pots and pans, the chatter of sous chefs, the rush of orders coming in and dishes going out. There's a rhythm, a harmony in this chaos. Now, picture a miscommunication. An order misunderstood, a dish mistimed. Suddenly that harmony is broken, the dance turns into a stumble, and the flames become a fire.

That kitchen, my friend, isn't much different from our everyday lives, especially in the high-stakes world of healthcare. Effective communication isn't just about getting the order right; it's about understanding the ingredients, the recipe, the palate of those we're serving. It's about dancing with clarity, grace, and empathy.

Enhancing communication skills isn't about who shouts the loudest or who has the last word. It's about finding the right balance between speaking and listening. It's not about being right; it's about being understood and understanding others. In the following pages, we'll explore the delicious art of **Effective Communication vs. Being Right**, where you'll discover that winning an argument might mean losing a connection.

And speaking of connection, have you ever felt the transformative power of being truly heard? **Active Listening and Compassionate Communication** are like the secret sauces that turn an ordinary dish into a culinary masterpiece. Whether it's with your colleagues or patients, a little sprinkle of empathy can bring out the flavors of trust, respect, and collaboration.

But what happens when the dish doesn't quite turn out right? When conflicts arise, and the kitchen gets hot? Fear not! **Navigating Challenging Conversations and Conflicts** is a recipe that will guide you through the tough spots with finesse and wisdom.

Are you tired of people being "upset" with you? A pinch of good communication will decrease that bitterness and add a touch of harmony. And when uncomfortable emotions in others threaten to spill over, you'll have strategies to ensure they don't become negative emotions in you.

Communication is more than words. It's a melody, a harmony, a dance. When you feel confident in your communication skills, you will unlock abilities to take risks, try new things, and deepen relationships. You won't feel stuck because you don't know how to speak up. You won't live in fear of the need for a difficult conversation because you will trust that you can navigate it with grace.

Effective Communication vs. Being Right

In our lives, especially in the healthcare setting, we often find ourselves in some form of debate. The stakes are high, and the pressure to be right, to have the answers, can feel like a boiling pot threatening to bubble over. But let's pause for a moment, shall we? Let's explore what it means to be effective rather than just being right.

Being right is ego. You are more concerned with demonstrating to the other person that you know more than they do or that your position is superior in some way. The goal of the communication is not focused on the best outcome, but on you making your point. When we can shift from this certainty that we are right into a mode of more curiosity, the interaction opens up and we have a more likely chance of successfully getting the message across.

Effective communication starts with active listening. Seek to understand where the other person is starting from. What is their understanding of the situation? What outcomes are most important to them and through what lens are they viewing the facts? Once you understand that, you can choose how to aim your words. If some of the facts are incorrect, you may address that. If you notice that they can get their "key outcome" without you having to sacrifice yours, propose this win-win situation and save the lengthy explanation of why you want what you want (they don't really care because they got what they wanted).

Let's think about a patient example. You are proposing a new treatment plan to a patient who is hesitant about it. You know you are right; the treatment is backed by evidence and proven to be effective. But the patient is scared, uncertain, clinging to old beliefs. You could insist on being right, pushing the treatment with facts and figures. But what if, instead, you choose to be effective? What if you listen to the patient's fears, acknowledge them, and then gently guide the conversation toward understanding and acceptance? That, my friend, is the gourmet dish of effective communication.

The first goal in effective communication is figuring out what you are actually talking about.

Imagine a colleague sharing her frustration about a procedure that went awry. You could interrupt, offer solutions, tell her where she went wrong. Or you could listen, truly listen, let her vent, empathize, and then gently guide her to her own insights. That's the five-star meal of compassionate communication.

Let's say you find yourself in a heated argument with a fellow healthcare provider over a patient's care plan. Emotions are flaring, words are flying out as each of you competes to make your point. What do you do? You turn down the heat. You breathe, you listen, you find common ground. You seek to understand before being understood, you build a bridge, not a wall.

The biggest definition of a successful negotiation in my book is if the other party walks away feeling like they "won" but you actually got everything you wanted.

So what does this communication stuff have to do with burnout? Plenty. Many of us essentially talk for a living and the stakes are high, the pressure is intense, and the demands are relentless. Practicing in a situation in which your skills are not matched to the challenge of the situation is one of the biggest drivers of burnout. Constantly feeling that you are struggling to perform. Imagine if a surgeon walked in day after day trying to perform a complex procedure they had never been properly trained to do. I can imagine that would lead to overwhelm and burnout in a hurry. Difficult conversations and complex interpersonal dynamics are not different. Navigating these situations requires communication skills, and many of us have never been trained. So learning some new communication skills that give you the tools you need to feel confident in every interaction will substantially diminish the mental load on you every day.

And remember, "communication" doesn't just mean the difficult or high-stakes conversations. Apply active listening and compassionate presence to lower stakes interactions. A little intentionality goes a long way to improving the day for yourself and those around you.

Imagine the nurse who listens, truly listens, to a patient's fears about a procedure. She doesn't rush, she doesn't dismiss; she connects. That connection doesn't just calm the patient; it feeds the nurse's sense of purpose, her joy in her work. It's a reminder of why she chose this path, this labor of love. It's a balm against the creeping burnout.

Consider the doctor who takes a moment to check in with a colleague, to share a laugh, a concern, an honest "how are you?" That's not just a polite conversation; it's a thread of connection, a reminder that they're in this together. It's a barrier against isolation, the exhaustion that can fan the flames of burnout.

Building strong and supportive relationships through communication is not just protective against burnout; it's like a sumptuous feast that feeds our passion, our empathy, our humanity. It reminds us that we're not alone in this kitchen, that we're part of a culinary dance that's richer, tastier, more satisfying when we cook and savor together.

Active Listening and Compassionate Communication

The tapestry of our relationships, especially in healthcare settings, is painted with the hues of vulnerability, trust, understanding, and empathy. It's not just about "getting along" with colleagues or being "good" with patients; it's about creating a realm of shared humanity. And boy, does it have its perks! Let's dive into the art and alchemy of relationship-building:

- Bare Your Soul (a little): Sharing snippets of our real selves can bridge divides. When we let our guard down, it signals to others that it's safe for them to do the same. Whether it's revealing your penchant for cheesy '80s music or your fear of spiders, it's these little quirks that make you relatable.
- Listen (and not just to reply): This is where our earlier lesson on active listening waltzes in. When you listen—truly listen—you're not just hearing words, you're receiving a part of someone's soul. It's a gift; treasure it.
- Express Genuine Appreciation: Ever received a heartfelt thank you? It feels like being wrapped in a warm blanket on a cold day. Be liberal with your

gratitude, especially with colleagues. Acknowledging the small deeds can solidify bonds.
- Create Shared Experiences: Remember those silly team-building exercises at work conferences? While they might seem clichéd, there's a method to the madness. Shared experiences, be it navigating a challenge or celebrating a success, are the adhesive in the relationship mosaic.
- Learn the Art of Apologizing: This isn't just about uttering the words "I'm sorry"; it's about recognizing when you've erred, understanding the impact of your actions, and genuinely seeking to mend the rift.
- Dabble in Different Worlds: Often, our relationships are siloed within our immediate circles. Step out. If you're a doctor, share a coffee with the janitors. If you're a nurse, join the IT team for lunch. Embrace the symphony of perspectives.
- Stay Present: In our multitasking world, giving someone your undivided attention is perhaps the most profound gift. It says, "In this moment, you matter the most."

Practicing Compassionate Communication When Things are Busy

For the skeptics who might be wondering, "Emma, in a high-stress environment like healthcare, who has the time for this?" Here's a revelation: building relationships isn't a time-consuming detour from your routine. It's an investment. Relationships can be the buoys that keep you afloat during turbulent times. They can shield you from burnout, infusing your workdays with moments of joy, understanding, and camaraderie.

Time is that ever-elusive ingredient in the bustling kitchen of healthcare. It slips through our fingers, leaving us feeling hurried, harried, and often overwhelmed. Can compassionate communication really save us time in this fast-paced world of beepers, buzzers, and never-ending to-do lists? Allow me to serve up some food for thought.

Imagine a rushed conversation with a patient, a hasty explanation that leaves them confused, scared, and resistant. Time saved? Perhaps a minute or two. But what about the lingering questions, the unspoken fears, the potential mistakes and misunderstandings that can bubble up later? The cost of your "efficiency" may be lingering confusion and mistrust, leading to more time-consuming interactions later.

Now imagine taking a breath, slowing down just enough to truly connect, to explain with empathy, to listen with care. It might take a few more minutes, but the clarity, the trust, the cooperative relationship that's built can save hours, days, even weeks down the line.

And what about our relationships with colleagues? That brief moment of connection, of checking in, of shared laughter or understanding isn't just a pleasant pause; it's the glue that binds a team. It's the oil that keeps the machine running smoothly, the seasoning that turns a bland task into a shared purpose. That time invested pays dividends in efficiency, in collaboration, in a workplace that hums with synergy and support.

Compassionate communication is not a luxury in a fast-paced world; it's the essential foundation that can turn chaos into calm, rush into rhythm, overwhelm into orchestration. It's the knowing touch that turns a hurried task into a healing art.

Time might seem like the scarcest resource in our hectic healthcare system, but compassionate communication is not the thief of time; it's the alchemist, the chef, the wise gardener that turns those fleeting moments into gold, into growth, into grace.

So let's not rush through our days like a hasty meal gulped down on the run. Let's savor, let's connect, let's dance in the flames and feast on the joy of being human, together. Let's trust that compassionate communication is not a drain but a wellspring, a source of time, of energy, of love. Let's believe that slowing down, just a touch, can actually speed us up, in ways that nourish not just our bodies, but our hearts, our souls, our very essence.

Relationship-building is akin to weaving a beautiful tapestry—each thread a testament to a moment shared, a laugh echoed, or a tear acknowledged. You see, in our rapidly evolving world, where digital interactions often eclipse face-to-face connections, the art of building genuine relationships seems almost vintage. Yet isn't it ironic that amid this whirlwind of technological marvels, our souls still yearn for authentic human connections, just as they did centuries ago?

I recall the time I found myself on a chaotic ward round, flanked by numerous healthcare professionals. We discussed patients with clinical detachment, sifting through notes, rattling off statistics. It was efficient, no doubt, but something felt amiss. It was during these rounds I met Jane, a senior nurse with laugh lines crinkling the corners of her eyes and a pocket full of Dove chocolates. She did something startling during a particularly intense discussion—she touched a distraught patient's hand, offering a genuine smile and a listening ear. In that simple gesture, I saw the magic of relationships unfold. Not just the clinical, textbook kind, but the raw, beautiful, deeply human kind.

Through her, I learned that every corridor chat, every shared joke, every moment of solace savoring a Dove chocolate was a thread, weaving the vibrant tapestry of our interconnected lives. As you navigate the intricate dance of your professional journey, pause occasionally. Look around. Cherish the relationships you're building. For in the end, it's these relationships that enrich our stories, adding depth, warmth, and iridescent colors to our life's canvas.

Active Listening and Compassionate Communication Exercise

Purpose:

This exercise aims to teach and practice the skills of active listening and compassionate communication. By engaging in these activities, you'll build stronger connections and enhance empathy in both personal and professional relationships.

Participants:

- Two willing participants (could be friends, family members, or colleagues)

Instructions:

1. Choose a Speaker and a Listener: Designate one person to be the Speaker, sharing their thoughts or feelings, and the other as the Listener, focusing on understanding and empathizing.

2. Pick a Conversation Starter: If needed, choose a topic or question that both participants find interesting. This can help spark a genuine and engaging conversation.

3. Speaker Shares: The Speaker begins sharing on the chosen topic, expressing thoughts, feelings, or experiences.

4. Listener Listens: The Listener's role is to fully concentrate on what the Speaker is saying. No

interrupting, no formulating a response, just attentive listening.

5. Reflect and Validate: After the Speaker finishes, the Listener reflects back what they've heard without judgment or advice. This helps the Speaker feel heard and understood.

6. Ask Open-Ended Questions: If the Listener wants to explore further, they can ask open-ended questions that encourage the Speaker to elaborate.

7. Swap Roles: Switch roles and repeat steps 3-6. This ensures that both participants experience both sides of the communication process.

8. Debrief: Spend some time discussing the experience. What was it like to truly listen? To be heard? Share insights and feelings about the process.

9. Practice Regularly: Make active listening and compassionate communication a regular part of your daily interactions. The more you practice, the more natural and rewarding it becomes.

Keep these key principles in mind:

- Patience: Take the time to truly hear and understand the other person.
- Curiosity: Approach each conversation with an open mind and a desire to learn.
- Empathy: Connect with the emotions and experiences behind the words.

Active listening and compassionate communication are essential tools in building meaningful connections. Whether with patients, colleagues, or loved ones, these skills promote understanding, trust, and empathy. Practice this exercise regularly to enhance your communication abilities and enrich your relationships.

10 phrases that can be valuable tools in your communication toolbox for practicing active listening:

1. "Can you tell me more about that?" - A great way to show interest and encourage the speaker to elaborate.

2. "It sounds like you felt..." - Reflecting back emotions helps the speaker feel understood and validated.

3. "I see what you mean, but I'd like to understand better how..." - Gently probing deeper while showing that you're engaged.

4. "I want to make sure I'm understanding you correctly; you're saying that..." - A way to clarify and confirm that you've grasped their point.

5. "That must have been really challenging/exciting/upsetting for you." - Expressing empathy toward their feelings.

6. "How did that experience affect you?" - Inviting them to share personal feelings and reactions.

7. "What was going through your mind when that happened?" - Encouraging them to share their thoughts or perspective.

8. "How would you like to see this situation resolved?" - Moving toward problem-solving while keeping their feelings and opinions at the forefront.

9. "I appreciate you sharing this with me. What can I do to support you?" - Showing gratitude for their openness and helping.

10. "Your perspective is really interesting. I hadn't thought of it that way before." - Acknowledging their unique viewpoint and appreciating the insight it provides.

Navigating Challenging Conversations and Conflicts

Communicating with Compassion: The Power of Nonviolent Communication

While the advice throughout this chapter provides a philosophical foundation for more compassionate communication, the Nonviolent Communication (NVC) framework offers a proven, practical methodology to transform how we understand and relate to ourselves and others. Developed by psychologist Marshall Rosenberg, NVC teaches us to identify and articulate our underlying observations, feelings, needs and requests in a way that fosters empathy, honest self-expression and positive relationships.

The four components of NVC are:

1. Observations: Stating the concrete actions and facts without judgment or evaluation. Instead of "You were so rude to me," an observation could be "When you raised your voice and walked away during our conversation…"
2. Feelings: Understanding how situations affect our emotions, using feeling words like happy, scared, frustrated.
"I felt hurt and disrespected…"
3. Needs: Recognizing the deeper needs, values and desires that are connected to our feelings, such as the need for trust, understanding or appreciation.
"…because I need to feel heard and valued in our interactions."
4. Requests: Clearly and consciously stating what we would like from the other person that could enrich our lives and meet our needs, without demands.
"Would you be willing to practice more patience, and hear me out fully before responding?"

In healthcare, applying NVC can dramatically improve how we navigate challenging situations with patients, families, colleagues and even ourselves. For example, when discussing a sensitive treatment plan, we could first make observations: "I've noticed you seem quieter than usual during this visit, and you looked anxious when I described the potential side effects." This opens the door to identifying and validating the patient's feelings and needs: "Are you feeling worried or overwhelmed? It's understandable to need extra reassurance about the pros and cons to make the best decision for yourself." From that place of empathetic understanding, we can make a request that attempts to meet both parties' needs: "Would you like to spend more time exploring all the options together so you can feel completely informed?"

NVC skills don't just improve our outward communication—they also cultivate deeper self-empathy and awareness of our own needs. We can turn the same framework inward, making observations about our internal experiences, naming how we feel, and getting curious about the needs underlying those feelings. This makes space for self-compassion and nurturing rather than harsh self-criticism.

Here are some examples of how the Nonviolent Communication framework can be applied in common healthcare scenarios:

1. Dealing with an upset patient:
   Instead of: "You're being completely unreasonable about this treatment plan."
   NVC approach:
   Observation - "I notice you seem agitated when we discuss the treatment options."
   Feeling - "I'm feeling concerned and wanting to understand your perspective better."
   Need - "Because it's important to me that we make decisions aligned with your values and goals."

Request - "Would you be willing to share what thoughts or fears are coming up for you regarding this plan?"
2. Receiving criticism from a colleague:
Instead of: "You're overreacting. My way was perfectly fine."
NVC approach:
Observation - "From your feedback, I understand you had some concerns about how I handled that situation."
Feeling - "I'm feeling defensive because I value doing good work."
Need - "And I have a need to feel supported by my colleagues."
Request - "Would you be able to provide more specific observations about what could be improved?"
3. Discussing end-of-life care with a family:
Instead of: "You need to accept that further treatment is futile."
NVC approach:
Observation - "I can see this is an incredibly difficult and emotional situation."
Feeling - "I'm feeling sadness watching your loved one's discomfort continue."
Need - "And I have a deep need to preserve dignity and minimize suffering."
Request - "Would you be open to exploring palliative care options to keep them comfortable?"

4. Negotiating schedule demands:
   Instead of: "You're being completely unreasonable with this workload."
   NVC approach:
   Observation - "The current scheduling expectations seem overly demanding."
   Feeling - "I'm feeling overwhelmed and fatigued trying to keep up."
   Need - "Because I have a need to sustain a healthy work-life balance and provide quality care."
   Request - "Would you be willing to discuss some flexibility or bring in extra support?"

The NVC process separates observation from evaluation, creates room for acknowledging feelings and needs on both sides, and allows for making clear, doable requests. This approach can defuse power struggles and adversarial dynamics that commonly arise in high-stress healthcare environments.

The NVC framework can also be immensely valuable for improving communication and collaboration within healthcare teams. Here are some ways NVC can be applied:

1. Building Trust and Psychological Safety
   NVC emphasizes empathic listening and making observations without judgment. This creates an environment where team members feel heard, understood, and respected—fostering trust and psychological safety to speak up.

For example, instead of saying "You're not prioritizing patient care" (which sounds accusatory), an NVC approach would be:

"I've noticed we've had to delay some patient discharges recently (observation). I'm feeling concerned (feeling) because providing timely care is really important to me (need). Would you be open to discussing how we can improve our discharge process? (request)"

2. Resolving Interprofessional Conflicts
   Healthcare involves professionals from diverse backgrounds working together. NVC helps navigate conflicts by separating observations from evaluations and focusing on mutual needs.

Instead of arguments like "Nurses never follow our orders properly," NVC allows expressing the root needs:

"When treatment orders don't get carried out (observation), I feel frustrated (feeling) because I have a need to ensure proper patient care (need). Would you be willing to explore a better system for communicating orders? (request)"

3. Giving Feedback Constructively
   NVC provides a clear framework for offering feedback that is specific, non-judgmental, and focuses on finding strategies that meet each party's needs.

Rather than "You're so disorganized," NVC-aligned feedback may sound like:

"I've noticed the supply area has been quite cluttered lately (observation). I'm feeling concerned about wasting time searching for items (feeling) because efficiency is important for good patient flow (need). Would you be open to suggestions for improving the organization system? (request)"

  4. Navigating Power Dynamics
     Healthcare teams have power imbalances between roles like physicians, nurses, techs, etc. NVC helps by removing language of demand, promoting mutual understanding.

Instead of orders like "Do this now!":

"It's now 3 p.m. (observation), and I'm feeling concerned (feeling) because updating records before handoff is crucial for continuity (need). Would you be able to prioritize documentation for now? (request)"

  5. Receiving Critical Feedback
     NVC teaches self-empathy to prevent feeling overtly defensive when receiving feedback. Responding from the NVC mindset opens pathways for growth.

Instead of denying issues brought up, one can respond:

"Thank you for bringing this to my attention (observation). I can sense I'm feeling defensive right now (feeling) because doing good work is very important to me (need). Would you be willing to provide some more specific examples so I can better understand the areas for improvement? (request)"

By integrating NVC practices, healthcare teams can build trust, reduce conflicts, give productive feedback, mitigate power struggles, and ultimately improve teamwork and patient care quality.

Maintaining Unconditional Positive Regard

An important piece of our compassionate communication framework is that we assume the other person has good intent. I utilize two powerful practices to help embody this mindset of unconditional positive regard prior to any difficult interaction.

Ho'oponopono

Ho'oponopono is an ancient Hawaiian practice of reconciliation and healing. The process is deceptively simple—you mentally repeat four phrases directed at the person you have tensions or upsets with:

"I'm sorry. Please forgive me. Thank you. I love you."

You can apply this to conflicts with loved ones, challenging relationships, or even just work through feelings toward someone you don't know personally but hold judgments against. The practice helps soothe wounds, release resentments, and restore an attitude of love and humility.

Although just four short phrases, allowing them to sweep over you with sincerity can be amazingly powerful for emotional healing and realignment. "I'm sorry" admits where you may have caused harm. "Please forgive me" asks for grace and a fresh start. "Thank you" expresses gratitude for the lessons learned. "I love you" reminds you of our shared humanity.

Ho'oponopono helps us take responsibility for our parts while developing empathy and compassion for the whole. It's the "MacGyver of emotional mending"—using just these few phrases to disarm conflicts and bring harmony into difficult relationships.

Metta Meditation

Another practice I use to cultivate unconditional positive regard is Metta, the Buddhist meditation on lovingkindness. You begin by directing loving wishes toward yourself: "May I be safe, healthy, peaceful and live with ease." You envision yourself bathed in warm wishes of kindness.

You then methodically extend that loving intention outward—toward loved ones, friends, mentors, then acquaintances, and finally even those you consider adversaries or sources of conflict. The phrases shift to "May they be safe… May they be peaceful…" You visualize each person surrounded by kindness.

What makes Metta so powerful is that it builds empathy for our shared human condition and desire for happiness. You cannot help but feel more understanding and goodwill, even toward those you currently struggle with.

Repeating these intentional lovingkindness phrases plants seeds of unconditional positive regard that can blossom into more gracious interactions.

Before engaging in any conversation where tensions may arise, I make every effort to first enter a mindset of empathy and compassion through these beautiful practices. They help soften my heart and see beyond surface conflicts to the shared hopes and positive intentions we all share, no matter our differences. Embodying unconditional positive regard in this way allows for more authentic and healing dialogue.

The Conscious Power of Silence

As we develop self-awareness, mindfulness, and boundary-setting skills, we must also learn to discern when conscious silence is the most prudent form of communication. The ancient teaching of the "Three Gates" offers guidance: Before speaking, we should filter our words through three gates: 1) Is it true? 2) Is it necessary? 3) Is it kind? If our intended statement does not pass through all three gates, it may be best to say nothing at all in that moment.

I often ask myself three key questions.

- Does this need to be said?
- Does it need to be said *now*?
- Does it need to be said *by me*?

This simple yet profound practice challenges us to look inward and ask: are my words truthful and accurate representations of reality? Do they serve a meaningful, necessary purpose beyond idle chatter or unconscious reaction? And ultimately, is my motivation one of authenticity and compassion rather than harmfulness or self-serving interest? If we cannot answer "yes" to all three criteria, then restraint and silence may be the wiser choice, at least temporarily.

Of course, there are times when speaking difficult but necessary truths with courage is appropriate and even ethical. The Three Gates simply prompt us to be more judicious and intentional with our speech. Instead of indiscriminate openness, we cultivate thoughtful discernment—knowing when to wield the power of words, and when to let silence speak most eloquently. With practice, this gate becomes a grounding force that allows us to respond vs. react, and to uphold truth and kindness as equal priorities.

This addition emphasizes that the communication skills introduced, like NVC, must be balanced with the wisdom to recognize when conscious silence is most skillful. It introduces the powerful Three Gates teaching as a guiding framework for that discernment.

The three fundamental questions about truthfulness, necessity, and kindness become filters we can "gate" our intended speech through. If our words do not pass through all three gates, then restraint and holding silence may ultimately be the most compassionate act in that moment.

It acknowledges there are absolutely times when truth-telling and difficult conversations are necessary. The Three Gates practice simply asks us to pause and speak more intentionally, rather than just indiscriminately blurting out every thought, reaction, or opinion that arises.

Used with integrity, the gates become an anchor for thoughtfully responding vs. unconsciously reacting. It balances priorities of being truthful *and* kind—not one at the expense of the other. With practice, this discernment allows us to wield the power of speech judiciously and let silence speak loudly when words could inadvertently cause more harm than good.

By learning to use our words wisely, we adopt the role of the firebreak that can halt a wildfire of verbal destruction. By adopting NVC skills we can take a step back and remain as calm as a seasoned firefighter in a five-alarm blaze. Firefighters rely on their training to navigate such stressful situations. NVC is the training you need to keep your cool. By speaking difficult but necessary truths with kindness, we harness the flames of vulnerability that burn away what constrains us, allowing new growth, resilience, and beauty to rise. With the skillful deployment of these tools, we become the wise fire guardians illuminating the path forward.

Although this may feel challenging at first, you will notice a difference in yourself when you adopt the principles on nonviolent communication and conscious silence. You will feel lighter and brighter, more consistently in-line with your deepest values and highest and best self. You will be more able to shine for yourself as well as those around you.

"Speak when you are angry, and you will make the best speech you will ever regret."

- Ambrose Bierce

CHAPTER 6
BECOMING A LIGHTHOUSE:
GUIDING OTHERS THROUGH THE FIRE

Have you ever met someone that it just felt good to be around? Someone whose warmth, energy, and positivity seemed to envelop you like a soothing embrace? The type of person who can brighten your disposition almost instantly, simply by being their authentic, radiant self?

I'll never forget the first time I met Joseph, an unwaveringly positive radiation technician at the cancer center where I worked and became a patient. As I anxiously awaited my appointment, Joseph bounded into the dreary waiting room, greeting each person with a huge smile and addressing many by name.

"Good morning, sunshine! Isn't it just a gorgeous day?" he cheerfully asked a frail elderly woman, whose face quickly transformed from a frown to a grin. With a gentle bedside manner, Joseph joked and swapped stories as he prepared people for radiation, putting even the most nervous patients instantly at ease.

Despite the inherently difficult environment he worked in, Joseph seemed to glide through the room like a soothing force, leaving a trail of laughter, lightness and optimism in his wake. I couldn't help but marvel at his ability to connect with people through simple acts of kindness and finding pockets of joy amid such sadness.

I asked Joseph how he could show up this way every day. He shared that he made it his personal mission to be an uplifting presence, believing that calming fears and raising spirits played a pivotal role in the healing process. "I get to be the first face they see before getting in the machine, so I want to bring them good energy," he explained. From that day on, I looked forward to my appointments, not just for the treatment, but for Joseph's restorative light that recharged my own resilience.

In healthcare and life in general, we all need those bright, soothing souls who seem to radiate optimism and elevate our spirits simply through their warm, caring presence. This chapter explores why these rare "lighthouses" are so powerful and how each of us can strive to be that beacon of hope for others.

I know you may be thinking, "Emma, I can barely get myself together, there is no way I can be a light for others." I used to think this way too—back when I was super burned out, I considered myself a danger to others. If I was at risk of flying off the handle and yelling at any given moment, I thought I should just lock myself in a cave so that at least I wouldn't injure anyone else in the process of melting down. Taking a step back and recognizing when you are in your crispiest moments is a good SOS skill and the reason we put rest and restore as a step on this path.

However, to fully heal, you need to recognize that people need you. You bring joy and light into the world simply by being you. So this healing journey gets you back to yourself so that you can shine this light that is already there inside you. This chapter paints the picture of why that is so important, not only for the impact it has on others, but on the compounding positive impact it will have on you. Showing up for other people, being an inspiration for others is nourishing. This is another example of the magical alchemy of giving something that actually increases the total amount of it. Just like love, gratitude, compassion, and kindness, when we share some light it actually makes more light in us.

So what does it take to be a lighthouse? Turn the light on.

I live in New England, so we have lots of those pretty old lighthouses that mark the entrances to harbors and coves and boats use to navigate.

Imagine you are a sailor in the days of yore. Lost, bewildered, beaten down by days at sea. And then you see it, the lighthouse beckoning you to your home harbor. This one sight immediately instills a sense of calm and hopefulness in you. I'm going to make it home!

Before there was GPS or other modern navigation tools, the lighthouse served as a beacon indicating "safe harbor this way." The lighthouse doesn't move or shout directions or know anything special about the place it stands, it just shines a light for other people to see. And in that way is incredibly beneficial to making sure sailors get to shore safely.

Okay, I'm going to drop the metaphor when we get to the part where we think about what happens if the lighthouse isn't on. I don't want you to have that pressure. This is just a metaphor, people. Get your head out of the "people will crash on the rocks if one day I don't feel well and can't turn on my light"—let's not catastrophize! But I do strongly believe that you showing up in your highest and best self (whatever version of it that is today) is a profound act of service even if you don't "do" anything else. The lighthouse fulfills its purpose simply being on. The lighthouse keeper knows the importance of keeping the light on and therefore takes action to ensure this.

Alright, let's come back from those idyllic New England shores for a moment and talk about some data.

Research on the positive feedback loop of being positive and surrounding yourself with positive people.

The power of positivity and surrounding yourself with uplifting individuals is not merely anecdotal; it's backed by substantial research in both business and psychology. Studies in organizational behavior have shown that a positive work environment can lead to increased productivity, creativity, and job satisfaction. Positive teams demonstrate higher engagement levels, greater collaboration, and are more likely to stay with their organization. Research by Dr. Barbara Fredrickson, a leading scholar in this field, introduced the "Broaden-and-Build" theory, which posits that positive emotions broaden one's awareness and encourage novel, varied, and exploratory thoughts and actions. Over time, this builds skills and resources for resilience and success.

Practicing Self-leadership: Being a Role Model in Self-care and Professional Behavior.

We often think of leadership as being the boss or manager. The person at the top. But true leadership is inspiring and supporting people in a way that allows them to be their best. Regardless of whether you are in a managerial position or you are a company of one, leadership is important. *Lead yourself first* is a common mantra and it means that you are the first one you need to inspire and support. By this point in this book you have a lot of tools to do this. Basically, doing stages 1-5 is self-leadership. Letting others see it is being a role model.

As you begin to develop your lighthouse skills, one thing you can do is talk about your self-care. What do you do to rest and restore, how do you establish boundaries, what have you learned in your journey of self-study? This doesn't have to be a formal presentation, moments of chitchat at the nursing station or while waiting for rounds to begin can be a time to share something positive. Most of the time these spaces are filled with complaints and venting frustrations. The simple act of saying something like "I got some really good sleep last night, I've been working hard on that and it is paying off" or "I'm excited about the yummy lunch I packed" can have immense positive ripples. I know, it is hard to believe that something so small could be so impactful, but it is! Maybe at first people will roll their eyes or give you an "okay, Pollyanna" kind of response. Let 'em, keep turning on the light, eventually those salty sailors will recognize it as the lifesaving beacon that it is.

The art of inspiring others: sharing your story and creating a vision.

Sharing your story can be scary. I mean your real story. Not the "can you believe this guy" or "I'm such a sad sack" stories we so often tell. Those stories are safe, they are really about someone else. Our story, the story of who we are and what is important to us is much more vulnerable. But these stories are the ones that are powerful. Having a clear story of who you are and why you do what you do is equally beneficial for you. Every time you tell it, it becomes a little truer. So go ahead and share that story about how you didn't get into med school on your first try and learned a little something about perseverance and not listening to haters. Or the story of how you intentionally choose your health over your comfort and get up every day to work out. Or even the story that one of those stories is what you wish you could tell, but you are still stuck in resentment that life seems so easy for other people.

We are all travelers on this path, everyone is at their own place. My challenge is to own your own story and let it light you up. If you look in the mirror and really don't like what you see (inside or outside), then do something about it. Staying negative and self-critical gets you nowhere. Stumbling in the dark may be where we find some important information about the light we seek, but we can't stay there. Make it your mission to be the light. Check in regularly on this mission. "How am I doing today on being bright and shiny?" "Do I need to tend to myself a bit so that I can brighten up?"

The mindset shift crucial here is to accept that keeping yourself bright is *the way* to accomplish everything you want.

This morning I had an early cross-country flight. Thousands of my fellow passengers and I were shuffling through the security line in our sleep-deprived haze. And then here is Terrance, the TSA agent checking my ID. Huge smile, quick joke, and clear instructions on where to go next. I made a comment that it was pretty good he was joking this early in the morning, and he responded, "Someone's got to bring the energy, right!" Damn, Terrance, way to serve me some of my own cooking. This guy understands what it means to be a lighthouse for those around him. I happened to be in a pretty decent mood (despite lack of coffee), but if I had been anxious or confused or overwhelmed, I sure would appreciate running into Terrance versus some grizzly, grumpy person who made me feel like a burden.

Here's the magic though, and why I am now addicted to this Bring Your Own Sunshine mentality. The sunnier you are, the more sunny-ly (word?) people respond to you. If you are constantly walking through life thinking, "Why can't more people be nice?", try being nice and sunny first. Start small, just a smile or good morning and see what response you get. As you get more comfortable you can start walking around telling people that they are awesome, and you are glad they are here. If you are feeling really crazy, say "I love you" to people outside your immediate family. This positivity game can get pretty fun if you let it.

Yes, you will be considered weird. We have a huge negativity bias and see "happy" people as somehow diseased. Check in with yourself if you feel this too. Get curious and see if there is some envy or shame masquerading here. If your brain is saying, "There must be something wrong with them, no one could be that happy," ask yourself why you believe that is true.

One reason we have such aversive reactions to happy people is because of the rampant toxic positivity, especially on social media. Toxic positivity is the idea that we must constantly maintain an outwardly positive veneer, no matter the circumstances. It stems from a societal pressure to remain relentlessly optimistic, downplaying or outright denying any struggles, negative emotions, or hardships we may face. This surface-level "happy face" invalidates the reality of human suffering and emotional complexity. Positivity without authenticity is more harmful than helpful.

True resilience isn't about plastering on a smile and pretending everything is okay. It's about developing the fortitude to properly work through painful experiences, allowing ourselves to feel and process the full range of emotions. Only then can we move forward with an authentic, grounded positivity. As we endeavor to shine light during dark times, we must be careful not to denigrate or dismiss the validity of personal challenges. Sustainable optimism comes from cultivating self-compassion, confronting harsh realities with honesty, yet maintaining hope by focusing on the light that still remains present.

Similarly, we have to resist the urge to go negative all the time. Human nature does tend to favor drama and negativity. It is a way to bond with those around us by identifying common suffering or a common enemy. Please believe that we can bond in positivity too! It is not impossible.

Supporting colleagues in their journey: building a culture of empathy.

Let's explore two more examples from vastly different industries, illustrating the pervasive influence of positivity across various domains.

1. **The Automotive Industry: Toyota's Collaborative Culture.** In the world of manufacturing and automotive production, Toyota stands as an example of how a positive, collaborative culture can lead to innovation and efficiency. The Toyota Production System (TPS), known for its "Lean Manufacturing" approach, encourages employees at all levels to contribute ideas for continuous improvement. This culture of positive reinforcement and open communication has been attributed to Toyota's consistent ranking as one of the world's most innovative companies.

2. **The Entertainment Industry: Walt Disney's Creative Environment.** The Walt Disney Company, one of the most recognized names in entertainment, thrives on a culture that fosters creativity, teamwork, and positive thinking. Walt Disney himself was known for his optimistic vision and his ability to inspire his team to think beyond conventional boundaries. Disney's "Blue Sky" brainstorming sessions encourage employees to contribute freely without judgment, cultivating an environment where positive collaboration fuels creativity. This has led to some of the most iconic and innovative products in the entertainment industry.

These examples from the automotive and entertainment industries emphasize that the benefits of a positive environment and attitude are not confined to a specific field. Whether in manufacturing cars or crafting stories, positivity plays a crucial role in fostering innovation, collaboration, and overall success. It offers a persuasive argument for healthcare professionals to adopt similar principles, focusing on positivity as a driving force in their daily practice.

Mentoring: Nurturing the Next Generation

As healthcare workers, we don't just treat patients—we also play a vital role in shaping and developing the newest members of our profession. How we mentor and guide students, interns, residents and younger staff sets the tone for their entire career trajectory and has reverberating impacts.

I'll never forget the soul-crushing experience as a student on my trauma surgery rotation. During intense patient rounds I used my hands to present the various body systems while presenting a case. One of the senior surgeons ridiculed me saying, "Quit waving your *bleep-bleep* hands, you are too *bleeping* cheery, it's unprofessional." His biting critique (not to mention profanity) embarrassed me in front of my peers and shattered my confidence. For days afterward, I could barely speak up coherently when presenting patients, gripped by fears of being mocked again for any perceived violations of cold professional decorum.

In that demoralizing moment, a seed of doubt was planted—that maybe I lacked the fortitude for this high-stakes field. That I didn't belong. All because I had displayed genuine enthusiasm and energy when discussing a patient's care. While that surgeon likely intended his harsh words as "motivation" in line with the more toxic hazing practices of the past, the impact could have derailed my entire career path.

We cannot allow such toxic criticism and antiquated power dynamics to persist in mentoring. It perpetuates a culture of fear, disillusionment, and burnout. The Yoga Sutras of Patanjali again offer instruction, "In relationships, the mind becomes purified by cultivating feelings of friendliness towards those who are happy, compassion for those who are suffering, goodwill towards those who are virtuous, and indifference towards those who are wicked." In this one line, we have the rules of engagement for how to respond to anything we may see from our trainees (really from anyone). If we interpret "purified" here as "lit from within" this gives us the roadmap for how to show up as a lighthouse every day. When we achieve a state where we are no longer clouded or darkened by judgments, we can shine most brightly. If that senior surgeon had followed these rules, I am sure he would have responded differently.

You may be thinking to yourself, but what about people who are truly doing wrong? We can't be indifferent when people make mistakes or behave unethically.

Here I would offer the concept of equanimity—maintaining an even-minded calm detachment rather than reacting with aversion or hostility toward those who act in unethical or harmful ways.

Equanimity does not mean apathy or condoning wicked actions. It's about not allowing yourself to be thrown off-balance emotionally or psychologically by the misdeeds of others. You maintain your own centered grace and compassion.

There are a few key reasons why equanimity toward the "wicked" is an important quality, especially for those in caring professions like healthcare:

1. It prevents you from being thrown off course or overwhelmed by toxic people/situations. You can remain focused on your higher principles rather than getting mired in negativity.
2. It allows you to respond with wisdom rather than being hijacked by anger or fear. You can better understand root causes and how to resolve issues.
3. By not meeting negativity with more negativity, you hold space for potential transformation in the person acting wickedly. Equanimity extends compassion.
4. It's a protection against burnout and cynicism. Equanimity helps you avoid internalizing or taking on the negativity directed at you.
5. It models the resilience and grace under fire that you hope to inspire in others facing darkness.

Ultimately, equanimity allows you to be the unwavering lighthouse vs. getting tossed around by every storm. You hold your higher ground perspective.

That said, it's incredibly difficult to maintain equanimity toward those who have caused real harm or trauma. It's an advanced practice that requires continually reinforcing the highest intentions of compassion and nonviolence, even for those who seem to lack those qualities themselves.

The key is not repressing natural human emotions like grief, anger, or a desire for justice to arise initially. It's about not allowing those emotions to perpetually run you—cultivating the steady inner balance to not get unmoored, so you can then take prudent action from that centered space.

The good news is that all the work we have done so far—cultivating intentional rest, establishing clear boundaries, developing a habit of self-inquiry, and crafting our communication skills—supports our ability to develop our equanimity muscles.

When we lead and uplift the next generation through compassionate nurturing, creating environments where they feel empowered to show up as their full, authentic selves, we set a virtuous example. As mentors, we must embody the ideal of unconditional friendliness and goodwill, devoid of pettiness or ego-driven hostility. Only then can we bolster their skills, confidence and resilience.

If for no other reason than our own self-interest, we should strive to be beacons of encouragement. After all, we want caring, grounded healthcare professionals to guide us through our most vulnerable moments when we inevitably become patients in need of their expertise and positive energy.

Resilience in Action: Showcasing Your Strength Amid Challenges

As lighthouses guiding others through storms, we in healthcare must embody resilience ourselves to inspire it in our patients and colleagues. But resilience isn't just an innate trait—it's a skill to be consistently nurtured and strengthened, especially amid difficult circumstances.

I'm reminded of a newly hired hospice nurse, Lisa, who was anxious about transitioning to caring for pediatric patients. Having only treated adults previously, she frequently voiced doubts about her abilities with children and conveyed feeling overwhelmed by the emotional weight.

Rather than criticize or dismiss her concerns, I made a concerted effort to "strength spot"—actively pointing out the powerful strengths Lisa leveraged in each patient interaction. After a particularly compassionate encounter, I praised, "Did you notice how you used your empathy strength to immediately put that child at ease? Your warmth allowed them to open up."

In another instance: "The creativity you showed in coming up with that imaginative hospice care plan was so inspiring. You channeled hopefulness in finding interactive ways to make their experience more joyful." Over time, my intentional strength-spotting helped Lisa gain awareness of the array of strengths she naturally possessed—empathy, emotional intelligence, creativity, hopefulness, bravery, kindness and more. Her eyes lit up with newfound confidence as she recognized the resilience and value she brought to the team.

Strength-spotting is a powerful practice for all of us to amplify our own resilience and positive capabilities. When we actively shine light on our strengths, we reinforce the helpful beliefs, mindsets and behaviors that arise from those strengths in challenging circumstances. Moreover, by strength-spotting in our colleagues and team members, we help them tap into their own deep wellsprings of resilience. A few impactful strength-based comments can be a catalyst for someone to find renewed passion and perseverance.

The more we make strength-spotting a habit, the more we reinforce resilience as learnable, growable qualities in ourselves and our teams. By seeing and appreciating the bright strengths that emerge from difficulty, we become empowered to rise above any darkness.

Here are some examples of specific strengths to call out in a typical healthcare setting.

Compassion

"You showed such deep compassion by staying late to comfort that family after their tragic loss."

"The compassion in your gentle voice and bedside manner provides so much healing."

Dedication

"Your dedication to meticulously researching all treatment options demonstrates your commitment to excellence."

"I'm in awe of your dedication—coming in on your day off to ensure seamless patient care."

Calm Under Pressure

"You radiated a calming presence during that chaotic emergency—your poise was invaluable."

"Even with limited resources, you handled that high-stress situation with remarkable composure."

Diligence

"The diligence you showed in those detailed follow-up notes will ensure nothing gets missed."

"I appreciate your diligent attention to sterilization protocols—it keeps us all safe."

Optimism

"Your optimistic spirit is like sunshine for our patients and the team."

"Staying hopeful and positive in the face of that setback is true optimism in action."

Attention to Detail

"Your meticulous attention to detail with that medication order prevented a serious error."

"The thorough and thoughtful way you documented those symptoms will really help with diagnosis."

Empowerment

"You empowered that patient by explaining things so clearly, giving them autonomy in their care."

"The way you advocated for this family and elevated their voice was empowering leadership."

Humility

"Your humility in admitting what you don't know and asking for help is a strength, not weakness."

"I appreciate your humble willingness to learn that new protocol despite being so experienced already."

The key is to shine light specifically on how you see each strength actively leveraged in their work, relationships, and perseverance through challenges. This makes the feedback more tangible and motivating.

Just as lighthouses stand as steadfast beacons guiding ships through tumultuous waters, we too are called to be unwavering sources of light and hope for those adrift in the churning seas of illness, trauma, and suffering. While radiating the life-preserving glow of our lighthouse ideals, we must also venture out as the guardians of ethical fire itself.

Like courageous firefighters, we will need to confront the insidious brushfires of politics and greed that currently scorch the ground so that equitable care and human dignity struggle to take root. As we brighten our lights, we must also leverage our influence to serve as firelines, to starve these spreading flames and protect the delicate ecosystems of progress struggling to thrive.

Participating in advocacy is no longer a choice. To fully realize our phoenix potential, we must engage in brave truth-telling. Our defiant songs awaken the yearning for a more enlightened world where all people can find their way to shores bathed in the warm light of compassionate belonging. While tending our lamp, we illuminate the path forward—clearing the way for new compassionate ecosystems to flourish and the promise of a better system for all.

"Be the lighthouse that guides others home when they've lost their way."

- Cleo Wade

CHAPTER 7
BATTLING THE BLAZE:
ADVOCATING FOR CHANGE TO EXTINGUISH SYSTEMIC BURNOUT

Imagine standing at the edge of a beach. You've built a magnificent sandcastle, paying attention to every delicate turret and wall. But as the tide comes in, waves threaten to wipe away your creation. No matter how intricately you've designed your sandcastle or how hard you try to shield it, the tide is coming in and the ocean is too powerful for you to overcome. This imagery mirrors the way individual desires and efforts can be washed away by systemic issues.

Consider these examples which highlight the impact of systems factors influencing the outcome despite the best intentions of the people involved.

The Lifestyle Change vs. The Concrete Jungle:

- *Individual Desire*: John, diagnosed with Type 2 diabetes, is motivated to turn his life around. He's been advised to engage in regular physical activity and eat fresh fruits and vegetables.
- *System Factors*: Living in an urban food desert, John's neighborhood lacks grocery stores that offer fresh produce. Instead, it's saturated with fast-food chains and convenience stores filled with processed foods. The parks, if any, are either too crowded, not well-maintained, or don't feel safe. The very environment in which John lives acts as a barrier to his health goals, making his path to a healthier lifestyle a steep uphill climb.

The Caring Nurse vs. The Clock:

- *Individual Desire*: Sarah, a dedicated nurse, takes pride in offering her patients compassionate and thorough care. She believes in spending those extra few minutes with each patient, ensuring they feel understood and cared for.
- *System Factors*: However, her hospital is constantly understaffed. The nurse-to-patient ratio is far from ideal, resulting in her juggling more patients than she can handle during her shift. Despite her best intentions, Sarah finds herself constantly racing against the clock, having to prioritize immediate medical needs over

personalized care. The system's constraints prevent her from offering the level of care she believes every patient deserves.

This is why having advocacy as part of your overall strategy is important. If you only focus on individual efforts, you will continue to have some element of frustration that you are not fulfilling your full potential. When you add in some advocacy efforts, you can rest assured that you are doing your part and contributing while also caring for yourself well.

I encourage very small advocacy efforts at first. I don't want the recently recovered to just jump into an intensive regimen of advocacy. I definitely don't want you to start self-criticism about your inadequate advocacy. What I do want you to do is notice and connect. Vote in elections at all levels of government and take a moment to reflect on the profound act that this is. Fill out a staff feedback survey or share an idea with your manager.

Many people have had negative experiences when "speaking up" in the past. One thing to consider is what state you were in when you spoke. When we act from a position of anger and frustration our words may not resonate well. This is why advocacy is the sixth step in this path. You need to get your house in order first. Keep your side of the street clean, as they say. We want to lead with love and compassion without excess attachment to the outcome. This is much more likely to be successful.

The other reason our efforts may fall short is that it just isn't the right time. Have you heard of the Apple Newton? Probably not. The Newton was released in 1993. It was one of the first personal digital assistants (PDAs) and a precursor to the smart phones we all love so much. The Newton had handwriting recognition and managed contacts, notes, and calendars. But the culture and technology of the early '90s were not fully prepared for such a device. Mobile computing was still a new concept, and many of the other technologies that make today's mobile devices so powerful (like touchscreens, fast processors, and high-density batteries) weren't yet available. More importantly, consumers did not recognize the need for such a device. No matter how good it was, it probably wasn't going to work because it wasn't the right time. Though the Newton was discontinued in 1998, the idea of mobile computing lived on. Apple eventually launched the iPhone in 2007, which has since become a game-changer in the way we live and communicate.

If you find yourself hitting the wall time after time, maybe it is not the time. Take a step back and consider the factors that may be far outside of your control that are affecting the outcome. Perhaps it is time to file that idea away for later and maintain your energy for when the time is right. Who knows if the iPhone would have been invented unless Apple had the perspective to drop the Newton and go back to the drawing board.

The US healthcare system is complex with many layers of dysfunction. By now you should understand numerous circumstances prevalent in this system contribute to healthcare worker burnout. I am not an expert in health policy or hospital management, so I won't go into detail about all the elements that could be improved. My goal in including advocacy as one of the core steps to overcome burnout is to help us all see what voice we do have. We need to avoid the overwhelm that comes when we think about "how to fix the system" and develop some strategies for keeping it local and making our voices count.

For some, this stage of the journey will involve advocacy on a grander scale. But very few of us will hold elected office or high-level leadership positions. The dynamic I want to recognize is the restorative power that being part of a movement for change has on us as individuals. Even very small acts, such as casting a vote or completing a feedback survey, improve our sense of agency.

In my work, I encounter a large burden of suffering every day. Children with life-threatening conditions, families who have spent every cent to care for their sick child, people with terrible cancers eating away at their bodies, and parents in grief after losing their child. These cases bring an emotional burden without much recognition. My work was measured in RVU and FTE. How many billable visits did you make? Can you be on call more nights this month? Can we start seeing outpatients too? For a people-pleasing, perfectionist, bleeding heart this is a recipe for disaster. So much suffering, so many people in need of help. I can learn how to maximize my billing to optimize my RVU, I will work more hours to see all the inpatients and a few outpatients per day (how can I say no), and call is really no problem. I just set myself up in a separate bedroom so that I don't wake my husband. Got it, sorted, no problem at all!

Without anyone there to stand up for me or put boundaries in place, I was perfectly willing to run myself ragged. We are conditioned for this through all our training. The patient comes first, life of sacrifice and service, doctors don't get sick, etc. I wish there had been someone at the top who saw the harms this mentality can have and put in some safeguards to keep people-pleasing, perfectionist, bleeding hearts like me safe. But there wasn't, so I crashed.

The other major systemic factor contributing to burnout in my case was the cultural disconnect between the work I was doing and the larger medical culture. As a palliative care provider, it is my role to understand the patient's narrative and goals and then advocate for a care plan aligned with those goals. We refer to this as goal-concordant care. In a paternalistic medical culture, doctors and nurses often feel that they know best and should make the decisions they feel are best for the patient.

This dynamic, coupled with the frequent psychology of overidentifying with the case and taking it personally if the patient dies, often led to clinicians being frankly antagonistic to the work I was trying to do. If they weren't antagonistic, they were often patronizing. "We know you are helpful to the patient, but we don't really need you here" was a sentiment I encountered regularly. The worst though, were the ones who wanted me to perform magic. "We are so excited to consult palliative care so you can come in here and make everything better." By the time they have placed this consultation, the patient is in multisystem organ failure, the family has hired an attorney, and the ICU team is all ready to quit. Without powers on par with Dumbledore's there is no way I am getting that situation tied up with a bow. In PC we love a good challenge and will certainly do our best to improve even the direst circumstances. What doesn't feel great is when our "colleagues" say things like "palliative care never helps" or "y'all really just made everything more complicated." These warm fuzzy statements really get you out of bed in the morning.

Too much work, uphill battles, and antagonizing parties are unfortunately the norm nowadays in healthcare. Recognizing all of these dynamics, I know now that I need to protect myself and establish my own boundaries. Now that I know there is no protector. Now that I know that my work may be met with criticism and adversity. Boundaries, focus on sphere of control, and intentional practices to counteract negative emotions are crucial to my sustainability in this profession.

But as I began to feel better, I realized how important it was to not only retreat into my own bubble, but also to speak up for change. We learned in the last chapter the power of showing up as a lighthouse. This is a form of advocacy and can be super impactful if linked to your intention to be part of the solution.

Witnessing injustices and recognizing they are outside your sphere of control is an important part of day-to-day sustainability. If we spend all our energy every day upset because we can't help in the way we wish we could, we are missing the opportunities to do the good work that is available to us. Focusing on the things that are in your control and letting go of the things outside is a key to sustainable practice. But what I have found is that medical professionals have a hard time letting go of the mission-driven, important-cause stuff that we witness. Having a little advocacy track in your life is like having a nice mailbox to post all the concerns you know you can't address at the moment.

One of my clients, Dr. B., found advocacy work to be very healing and grounding. Dr. B. is a general pediatrician in a busy practice that serves a large urban area. She experienced burnout related to the large number of patients who needed care, but also from the overwhelm she experienced caring for people with so many unmet basic needs. She had a profound sense of hopelessness that nothing she did really mattered. She was ready to quit and felt that all her knowledge and training were useless in the face of such monumental problems in the world. Her purpose and mission is to care for children so that they could grow into healthy and thriving adults. We worked together to create some systems for her to recognize the good work she was doing day-to-day as well as find connections so that she could impact changes on a broader scale. We started by focusing very narrowly on her sphere of control and then worked outward to increase her sphere of influence.

For Dr. B., this initially meant focusing daily on the impact of her clinical practice. The bread and butter of pediatrics, well child visits, and routine vaccinations were framed as the cornerstones of keeping kids healthy and safe. Implementing systems within her practice to keep more kids on track was something she had control over. Keeping her focus on things close to home was also something she had control over. A low media diet was a big part of her recovery. For Dr. B., taking intelligent action required that she tune out some of the constant negative news cycle.

She also had control over her mindset. One key shift for her was shifting from aggravation with the "worried well" to an appreciation that these visits were opportunities to support parents in developing their own agency and self-confidence, which would in turn help them to raise their children well. These steps helped her a lot and she regained a large part of herself form these steps alone. But she called me one day and said, "There still seems to be something missing, I still feel like I'm not doing enough."

For Dr. B., seeing how her little corner of the world fit in to a greater context was empowering, but she didn't feel complete without knowing she was doing something to change the broader story. Her advocacy journey began with what we initially called the "grievance notebook," which was a place for her to capture all the things she witnessed that were outside of her control. I encouraged her to really capture it all. We would come back to it later and decide which pieces of this might be hers to work on.

Knowing that she didn't have a lot of time to take on a major initiative, she joined her local chapter of the AAP and state medical society. Through participation in these groups, she is able to funnel her "grievances" to organizations empowered to advocate at a larger level. She also makes it a point to vote in all elections at all levels and knows how to contact her representatives.

As a result of these shifts, Dr. B. now goes to work each day energized. She has confidence that she is helping people and leaves work every day knowing she has done enough.

Bright Spots and Success Stories

The Dr. Lorna Breen Healthcare Provider Protection Act was signed into law in 2022, providing grants for training healthcare providers in strategies to reduce burnout and improve mental health. The Lorna Breen Foundation runs a free online support group for healthcare workers facilitated by mental health professionals. The foundation is named after Dr. Lorna Breen, an emergency room physician at New York-Presbyterian Allen Hospital, who died by suicide in April 2020 after contracting COVID-19 and returning to the front lines treating patients during the peak of the pandemic in New York City. Her family turned grief into advocacy, using the tragedy of her death to shine a light on the crisis of burnout and mental health among healthcare workers, especially amid the turmoil of COVID-19.

At Cincinnati Children's Hospital, advocacy efforts over several years paved the way for the creation of a chief wellness officer position in 2023. For many years there was a band of advocates clamoring for more support and wellness services. Early successes included the initiation of Schwartz center rounds and the development of a peer-to-peer support program. The group struggled to get traction until 2022, when a leadership change brought in new leaders who seemed more invested in developing more robust wellness programs. Advocates capitalized on this change to encourage participation as a pilot site for the Healing Healthcare Initiative through the Schwartz Center.

Through this initiative, which allowed leaders to learn about becoming a trauma-informed organization, the stage was set. In early 2023, a dedicated and unwavering physician took the reins and made the pitch for a formal chief wellness officer role. By July 2023, the position was created, and the new wellness officer began work. This success demonstrates the importance of perseverance from advocates, recognizing opportune timing with leadership transitions and the vital role of institutional leadership prioritization in substantively advancing healthcare workforce well-being initiatives.

There are several other notable organizations and initiatives working to address burnout and promote mental health among healthcare professionals:

National Organizations:

- The National Academy of Medicine's Action Collaborative on Clinician Well-Being and Resilience - A network of organizations committed to promoting clinician well-being as a national priority.
- The American Medical Association's Practice Transformation Initiative - Provides resources and training focused on professional well-being.
- The American Nurses Association's Healthy Nurse, Healthy Nation initiative - Connects nurses with resources for mental health, nutrition, physical activity, and more.
- National organizations focused on specific sectors like emergency medicine physicians, surgeons, etc. also have well-being initiatives.
- Healthcare System Programs:
- Many major healthcare systems like Cleveland Clinic, Stanford Healthcare, and Mass General have launched comprehensive well-being programs and chief wellness officer roles.
- Initiatives focused on counseling services, peer support programs, mindfulness training, process improvements to reduce burnout drivers like charting time.

- Academic Programs:
- Medical schools and nursing programs increasingly have curriculum covering self-care, resilience, and coping strategies for burnout.
- Researchers studying interventions, systemic contributors to burnout, and outcomes measurement.

While more progress is still needed, these organizational efforts signal an increased prioritization around supporting the mental health and well-being of healthcare workers in the face of rising burnout levels.

How to Get Started

The key is finding your VOICE.

V.O.I.C.E.

V - Validate your feelings and experiences. Recognize that your perspective, rooted in your unique experiences and observations, holds immense value. Your feelings and insights are the foundation of your advocacy efforts.

O - Organize your thoughts and gather data. Before approaching others with your concerns or ideas, take a moment to collect your thoughts, gather supporting evidence, and anticipate questions or counterarguments. Being organized gives your advocacy efforts a solid foundation.

I - Initiate conversations. Begin dialogues with colleagues, superiors, or community members. Share your concerns, insights, and hopes. Remember, the first step toward change is often simply starting the conversation.

C - Collaborate with allies. Seek out like-minded individuals who share your concerns or vision. There's strength in numbers, and together, you can amplify your message and create a more significant impact.

E - Empower yourself and others. Recognize that advocacy isn't just about seeking change; it is about empowering yourself and others to believe in and fight for a brighter, more inclusive future. Celebrate small victories, learn from setbacks, and continually inspire those around you to join the movement.

Using the V.O.I.C.E. acronym, anyone can remember that advocacy is not a distant or unattainable goal but something accessible, practical, and rooted in everyday experiences and actions.

If you don't feel that starting an initiative or speaking out is right for you, what can you do? One thing we can all do is commit to listening and learning. When we hear about a push for change, can we meet it with curiosity and open mindedness? The mindset and heartset that says "tell me more about this" instead of "it will never work" or "we've tried that before." Be willing to take a step back and learn more about an idea before deciding that you don't like it or jumping into fear about how that change might upend your life. As we said earlier, it is unlikely that we have a solution that will make everyone happy. Be and advocate by holding some space for the ideas of others.

I see you and I see what you are trying to do. Thanks for trying. Recognize the power in just showing up day after day to take intelligent action and support the intelligent actions of others. Make a habit of recognizing the incremental work that is being done and trust the process.

The metaphor I love for intelligent daily action is of growing a flower. Intelligent actions are to prepare the soil well, plan the seed at the proper depth, water appropriately, place your plant in an area that gets proper sun, and protect your baby plant from predators. Unintelligent actions would be digging up the seed every day to see if it has sprouted, or watering it excessively, or ripping the bud apart to make it "bloom faster." Any of these actions will likely kill the plant (or at least ruin the flower) and take you further from your mission of growing a flower. Even if you do all the right actions, you may not get a flower. That is how life is sometimes, but you will know you did everything possible to nurture it. If instead you had become overwhelmed by the difficulty of growing a flower and stopped watering it because it probably wouldn't grow anyway, you are failing to take action and therefore will not achieve your mission.

The Phoenix's Advocacy Approach

Like the mythical phoenix, some advocates are called to uplift the human narrative and rekindle the soulful essence of why we became healers. Through narrative medicine, medical humanities efforts, and compassionate listening campaigns, the phoenix reminds us of the artistry in attending to the human condition and honoring each person's unique story.

The phoenix advocates by giving voice to suffering often silenced—lifting up marginalized perspectives, validating lived experiences dismissed, and fanning the embers of our shared hopes for dignity and understanding. They use their creativity and truth-telling voices as the spark that clears space for healing to take root in new, more holistic ways.

The Firefighter's Advocacy Approach

While the phoenix sings its soulful melodies, the firefighter advocates focus on protective policy reforms, systemic accountability measures, and public education as "fire mitigation strategies" against the smoldering injustices threatening to ignite into uncontrolled conflagrations.

The firefighter's focused prevention and containment efforts work to reinforce firelines—strengthening institutional standards, reporting mechanisms and legislation that can starve discrimination, profiteering, and unethical practices of oxygen before they can rapidly spread. Their proactive approach, rigorous training protocols, and enforcement aim to create an environment fire-resistant to corruption taking ruinous hold.

Spheres of Control Exercise

While the phoenix and firefighter operate with different methodologies, both derive power from clarity on what spheres they can actively influence. An empowering exercise is mapping your spheres of control:

1. List situations, policies or injustices over which you have direct control to create positive change.
2. Next, list areas where you have influence, even if not ultimate authority.
3. Finally, list circumstances largely outside your control, beyond your sphere of impact.

The most constructive advocacy efforts focus on spheres 1 and 2—areas you can meaningfully affect through your voice, efforts, and platforming of others. Sphere 3 situations, while unjust, must be accepted with grace to avoid exhausting yourself fruitlessly.

Consistent action within your spheres of control, amplified by strategic partnerships/coalitions within your spheres of influence, slowly expands the territory where you can impact change. Patience, resilience and adaptability are the firefighter's and the phoenix's shared virtues.

Now that you know the six core steps to overcoming burnout, you are ready to get super creative and build your communities. Read on to learn about the treats you have in store. Recovering from burnout is a bit like peeling an onion. Layer by layer you learn a bit more about yourself, you build stronger boundaries, you deepen community connections, and you become an even more powerful agent of change.

"Never doubt that a small group of thoughtful, committed citizens can change the world; indeed, it's the only thing that ever has."

- Margaret Mead

CHAPTER 8
IGNITING YOUR CREATIVE GENIUS:
FANNING THE FLAMES OF INNOVATION

Imagine a world where every problem has a creative solution waiting to be discovered, where the limitations we perceive are merely invitations to think differently.

My initial concept of how creativity fit into this whole burnout recovery scheme was that it was the result. When you made it through all the steps you would find creativity. It was the reward for going through the work.

This is correct in some ways and very wrong in others. The sense that creativity is what we are "chasing" is probably right. Being creative feels great. The opportunity to have new ideas, to try them out, to feel that spark of inspiration. Those are such deeply human elements that resonate with everyone. People who say "I'm not creative" either have too narrow a definition of creativity or have forgotten how.

So it is the "goal" in that way. Do the steps—rest, self-study, boundary, communicate, shine for others, advocate—and get your dessert of creativity! But it is also part of the path. Tapping into our creative side gives us power and infuses all the other things we do with more joy. To do this, all we need to do is widen our view of what it is to "be creative" and make a little intention to do creative things regularly.

Redefining Creativity

What does it mean to "be creative?" You may immediately think about artistic expressions such as painting, music, dance, or writing. Certainly, there is creativity involved in these things (and a lot of technical, repetitive, and boring parts just like any other activity) but there are so many more ways to exercise creativity. Letting your mind wander and having an interesting idea is a creative act. This could be as simple as taking a different route to work and noticing the new buildings you pass along the way. Or messing around in the kitchen and coming up with a new dish. Or thinking up a new process to help you carry out some daily task with more efficiency or fun.

Teaching certainly involves a lot of creativity. Approaching a complex topic and figuring out how to break it down into understandable parts and then think about how to present those parts in an engaging way—so many creative opportunities! Communication in general has endless opportunities for creativity. For example, you could get creative with your email signature. Leave an inspirational message or succinctly describe your mission statement or hype up a new project you are working on. I have a friend who always leaves a playlist in her out-of-office message! Lots of fun ways to play around there.

In-person communication offers endless possibilities as well. Consider a patient encounter in which you are providing some lifestyle counseling to help your patient address their hypertension and hyperlipidemia. Using your creativity, you artfully ask questions to elicit the patient's values which serve as the hooks to hang your recommendations on. Then you can both be creative together in developing solutions or strategies to help them achieve their goals. Instead of feeling drained that you had to talk about diet and exercise for the 110th time this week, you feel energized that your creative expression was beneficial for your fellow human. See how all this stuff works together!

So now that we see there are lots of ways to be creative, you may already have shed the "I'm not creative" myth. If that belief still seems to be hanging on, let's do a little exercise to clear it out. Remember to keep it EASY.

Unleashing Your Creative Potential: A Guided Exercise

Objective: To dismantle the belief "I'm not creative" and unlock the creative potential that lives within you.

Materials Needed: Paper, pen or pencil, colored markers or crayons (optional), a quiet space.

Time Required: 15-20 minutes.

Instructions

1. Reflect on the Belief: Write down the statement "I'm not creative" on the top of your paper. Spend a moment reflecting on why you might hold this belief. Jot down any thoughts or memories that come up.

2. Challenge the Belief: Beneath your first statement, write down three instances where you've been creative in the past. Think broadly; creativity doesn't have to be related to art or music. It can be in problem-solving, communicating, organizing, etc. If you're struggling, consider the times you've found unique solutions to problems at work or at home.

3. Create a Positive Affirmation: Replace the negative statement with a positive affirmation, such as "I am creative in my unique way." Write this down and decorate it if you like. Allow yourself to feel the truth in this statement.

4. Engage Your Creativity: Now, turn to a blank page and let your creativity flow. Sketch, doodle, or write a poem or a short story. Let your hand move freely without judgment. It doesn't have to be a masterpiece, just let it be an expression of you. If you struggle with perfectionism, do this with your nondominant hand, this releases the expectation that it will look "good." If art is not your thing, let your creative juices flow to make up a song, create a skit, or even redecorate your living room.

5. Reflect: Look at what you've created. Acknowledge the creativity that went into it. It's proof that creativity is within you.

6. Daily Practice (Optional): For the next week, take five minutes each day to repeat this exercise, especially the creative engagement part. Allow yourself to explore different creative avenues.

This exercise aims to shatter the limiting belief that you are not a creative person, revealing the boundless creative potential that resides within you. By challenging the negative self-talk, engaging in a hands-on creative activity, and reflecting on the process, you've taken the first step toward embracing your creative genius. As you continue to nurture this aspect of yourself through daily practice, you'll unlock a profound sense of joy and fulfillment. Creativity is not just a means of self-expression but also a gateway to tapping into the deepest sources of joy in your life. In the next section, we'll explore how to identify and cultivate these unique drivers of joy, allowing you to live a life infused with purpose, passion, and an unwavering sense of well-being.

The Pursuit of Joy

What is joy? By their very nature, experiences of joy are hard to articulate. We may think of an intense feeling of deep spiritual connection, pleasure, or appreciation. Brené Brown defines it as a *good mood of the soul.* You may call to mind some events such as the birth of your first child or your wedding day as representations of joy. I want to suggest that joy is a feeling we should access regularly and in everyday circumstances as much as possible.

Tapping into joy regularly requires that we name our drivers of joy. Those are the core beliefs and values that we tether our joy to. In my book (you know, the one you are reading), joy is different from happiness. This is just a way to use words as there is no academic consensus on what any of these terms mean. I think of happiness as more of a surface experience that may be tied to circumstances. I feel happy when things are going my way and I am getting things I want. Of course, we want to feel happy, and there are many frameworks that use happiness as the peak outcome. But I have seen too much sadness and suffering for this to make sense to me, so I go for joy. I think that my soul can still be in a good mood even when I am sad, anguished, or disappointed. By connecting into my drivers of joy, I can keep this joyful quality even amid difficult circumstances.

Let's take a moment to find some of your unique sources of joy.

Identifying Your Unique Drivers of Joy

Objective: To reflect on the various aspects of your life that bring you joy

Materials needed: journal/paper and pen/pencil

Time required: 10-20 minutes

Instructions: Part 1. Review the following prompts and make an initial list of things in your life that bring you joy. Be open and honest with yourself as you fill out each section. Remember, joy can come from both big and small things, so capture all the aspects that resonate with you.

1. Activities and Hobbies: List the activities, hobbies, or pastimes that bring you joy. These can be things you currently engage in or those you used to enjoy but haven't made time for recently.

2. Relationships: Identify the people in your life who bring you joy and happiness. These can be family members, friends, colleagues, or anyone else who positively impacts your well-being.

3. Places and Environments: Consider the locations or environments that uplift your spirits and bring you a sense of joy. These can be physical places or settings where you feel most comfortable and inspired.

4. Accomplishments and Milestones: Reflect on your personal achievements and milestones that have brought you a sense of joy and fulfillment. These can be both professional and personal accomplishments.

5. Values and Beliefs: Think about the values and beliefs that resonate with you on a deep level. These can be guiding principles that bring you joy when you live in alignment with them.

6. Moments of Serenity and Peace: Recall the moments when you feel at peace, calm, and content. These can be

moments of solitude, mindfulness, or connection with nature.

7. Unexpected Joys: Consider the things that unexpectedly bring you joy and put a smile on your face. These can be small surprises, acts of kindness, or simple pleasures.

8. New Experiences: Think about the new experiences you've had or those you would like to have that bring a sense of excitement and joy. These can be adventures, learning opportunities, or stepping out of your comfort zone.

Reflection:

Take a moment to review your responses. Notice any patterns or recurring themes among your drivers of joy. Reflect on how you can incorporate more of these elements into your daily life and prioritize activities, relationships, and environments that bring you joy.

Remember, joy is a personal and unique experience. Embrace and celebrate the things that bring you joy, as they play an essential role in creating a fulfilling and balanced life.

Part 2. Connect your experiences of joy to two to five broad themes. Use the themes suggested below or create a theme in your own words. These joy themes will serve as anchors for your actions and connecting what you do every day to your deeper meaning and purpose.

1. Creativity and Expression: Engaging in artistic pursuits, exploring creative outlets, and expressing oneself through various mediums.
2. Connection and Relationships: Building meaningful connections with loved ones, fostering deep relationships, and experiencing the joy of shared experiences.
3. Nature and Outdoors: Connecting with the natural world, spending time in nature, and appreciating the beauty and tranquility of outdoor environments.
4. Personal Growth and Learning: Pursuing personal development, expanding knowledge, and experiencing joy through continuous learning and self-improvement.
5. Mindfulness and Presence: Cultivating a sense of mindfulness, being fully present in the present moment, and finding joy in the simple pleasures of life.
6. Acts of Kindness and Service: Performing acts of kindness, helping others, and contributing to the well-being of those in need.
7. Adventure and Exploration: Seeking new experiences, embracing adventure, and stepping out of comfort zones to discover joy in the unknown.
8. Laughter and Humor: Enjoying moments of laughter, finding humor in everyday situations, and embracing lightheartedness and joyfulness.

9. Wellness and Self-Care: Nurturing one's physical, emotional, and mental well-being, and finding joy through self-care practices that promote balance and vitality.
10. Gratitude and Appreciation: Cultivating a sense of gratitude, appreciating life's blessings, and finding joy in the simple joys and everyday moments.

No worries if you did this exercise and thought to yourself, "I love all of that!" Great, it is wonderful to have so much joy in your life. The main objective and beauty of this exercise is to help you see it and give you some language around it.

Now you can connect everything you do to something that brings you joy. All the stuff of life can move from *have to* or *should* to *get to* or *tapping my joy.* Little bitty change in words, huge shift in mindset!

Some suggestions for strategies to tap into your drivers of joy based on the themes you identified.

1. **Creativity and Expression:** Sketching a picture with your children during a weekend family art session or writing in a journal in the evenings to reflect on your experiences both in your professional life and as a mom.
2. **Connection and Relationships:** Scheduling regular family dinners to build and maintain strong connections with your partner and

children or hosting monthly gatherings with fellow physician moms to foster a supportive community.
3. **Nature and Outdoors:** Taking a morning jog in the local park before your hospital shift or planning family hiking trips on weekends to help your children explore and appreciate the natural world.
4. **Personal Growth and Learning:** Attending a medical conference or online workshop to stay up to date with the latest medical advancements, or reading books related to parenting or personal interests to encourage continual growth.
5. **Mindfulness and Presence:** Practicing a ten-minute morning meditation to start your day centered and focused or setting aside phone-free time with your children to fully engage with them.
6. **Acts of Kindness and Service:** Volunteering at a local community health fair to provide free checkups or baking cookies with your children to deliver to a neighbor in need or a colleague at the hospital.
7. **Adventure and Exploration:** Trying a new sport with your family like rock climbing or planning surprise outings to unfamiliar local attractions to foster a sense of adventure.
8. **Laughter and Humor:** Sharing a funny story with your patients to lighten the mood, or watching a comedy show with your partner after the children are asleep to unwind and laugh together.

9. **Wellness and Self-Care:** Setting a strict bedtime routine to ensure sufficient rest or scheduling a regular spa day or quiet reading time to nurture your emotional and mental health.
10. **Gratitude and Appreciation:** Keeping a gratitude journal to write down small joys every day or starting a family tradition of sharing something you're grateful for during dinner to encourage appreciation for life's simple joys.

This exercise has guided you through a deep exploration of the unique drivers of joy in your life. By reflecting on the various activities, relationships, environments, and experiences that bring you happiness, you've gained a clearer understanding of what truly fulfills and energizes you. As you incorporate more of these joy-inducing elements into your daily routine, you'll find yourself experiencing a heightened sense of engagement and focus—a state known as "flow." In the next section, we'll delve into the concept of flow and explore strategies to cultivate this optimal state of energized focus, where time seems to dissolve, and you fully immerse yourself in the present moment. Achieving a state of flow not only enhances your overall well-being but also unlocks a deep sense of creativity, productivity, and personal growth.

Flow State – Finding Your Energized Focus

Being in flow state is a psychological experience when one is performing an activity in which you are fully immersed with an energized focus. Sounds pretty good, right? Evidence shows that time in flow state contributes to well-being and personal fulfillment. Increased flow experiences lead to increased intrinsic motivation, self-esteem and time spent doing meaningful work. In a professional context, finding flow can lead to higher productivity and innovation, as evidenced in various studies across fields ranging from arts and sports to business and science.

Flow is not only beneficial for individual growth and performance but also plays a vital role in team dynamics and collaboration. Research has shown that teams can experience a collective flow state, leading to synergistic creativity and problem-solving. In healthcare and other demanding fields, the ability to achieve flow could contribute to improved patient care, team communication, and overall work satisfaction. Whether individually or collectively, the experience of flow represents a powerful avenue for personal and professional development, offering a path to heightened focus, creativity, and fulfillment.

Activities that put you in the flow state are in the sweet spot between boredom and anxiety. They need to be challenging enough to be engaging but not so hard or far outside of your skill level that you shut down.

Elements of being in flow:

- An intensely focused concentration on the present moment and a loss of relative self-consciousness.
- A sense of deep focus and effortless involvement that makes other needs negligible.
- The experience that action and awareness are merged.
- Intrinsically rewarding activity.
- Immediate feedback on the progress as the participant engages in the activity and the belief in potential success.
- Clear goals.
- No concern about the judgment of others.
- A sense of personal control or agency in the activity.
- A sense of distortion of time (e.g., time seems to slow down or pass quickly).

Think of a time when you were completely absorbed and focused. This could be at work, but it is often easier to think about a leisure activity or hobby. Examples may be swimming, table tennis, yoga, tai chi, cycling, running (especially trails), hiking, rock climbing, baking, crafts. Take a moment to recall that feeling of absorption. Singular focus on the task at hand was effortless because you were in the flow.

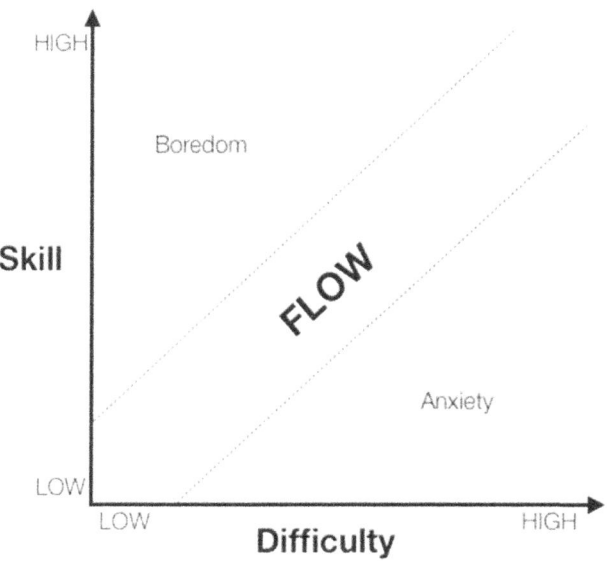

Why do I present this discussion of flow state and joy in this chapter about creativity, and what does all of this have to do with burnout? Because when we are feeling creative and open, we can access these states more easily. All the work from the prior steps leads you here. To this magical state of joy and flow. This allows you to work while still feeling in control and under control. You are neither anxious nor bored and there is always a clear line of sight between what you are doing and your unique drivers of joy. No matter what shit show is thrown in your path, you, my friend, will navigate with ease.

Okay, so now we know that there are so many ways to be creative and to creatively find joy in our day-to-day experiences. To deepen this understanding, I want you to do something different. Have the confidence to try something unexpected, to go off topic. It will enhance your primary mission in amazing ways.

I want you to play, to feel the way it feels to do something a little outside your norm. To do something with no real *purpose* in the traditional sense (of course it has a purpose in your journey of personal development!).

Pick an activity that is interesting to you but outside your comfort zone. Ideally something that engages you to move or use your hands. We want some of that body memory getting involved here. This could be baking, cooking, making crafts, doing a sport, playing music or writing poetry. Try the new thing. You can spend a little time in learning mode, looking up a recipe or watching a

YouTube instructional video, but don't get stuck in learning, get on with it. Do the thing. Let it be weird. Play around with it. If you get stuck, get creative on how you can get back into flow. Just enjoy the sheer joy of doing something different. What if this moment didn't need to be anything other than what it was?

Maybe you will love this new activity and decide to practice it more. Maybe you will never do it again. This is not the point; the point is to *play*. Do something for the fun of it, for exploration, for creativity. This is good for your brain.

The Creative Mindset: Chasing Purpose, Not Perfection

When we can put ourselves into this creative mindset and allow ourselves to play, we allow ourselves to find purpose. The pursuit of perfection and the fear of messing up can really keep us from achieving purpose.

I have watched countless friends and colleagues lose their amazingness under the cloud of perfectionism. A large part of our burnout epidemic is driven by this lack of purpose and deep fulfillment. The story of Dr. O is one that is all too familiar, yet still makes me sad every time I hear it.

Dr. O is an exceptional physician (and person). We met after she quit her job in the ER and was looking for help finding her path. "I just don't love it anymore, and I don't know what else to do." Looking back over her journey, we were able to understand together the role that perfectionism played in her demise.

Dr O had always been an exceptional student, driven to excel in every aspect of her medical training. As a young intern, her relentless pursuit of perfection fueled her creativity and innovation in the field of emergency medicine. She loved the challenge of piecing together the puzzle of a patient's symptoms, drawing on her vast medical knowledge to devise novel treatment plans. She would spend hours brainstorming new approaches, invigorated by the prospect of improving outcomes and pushing the boundaries of what was possible in her specialty.

Her colleagues were inspired by her analytical nature and her ability to think outside the box. Patients were drawn to her warm bedside manner and the genuine care she showed for their well-being. In those early days, Dr. O felt a deep sense of purpose and fulfillment in her work—this was her calling, the place where she could truly make a difference. But over time, the unforgiving drive for perfection began to take its toll. She would agonize over every decision, paralyzed by the fear of making even the slightest mistake. She became obsessed with anticipating and mitigating every possible risk, second-guessing herself at every turn.

The spontaneity and joy that had once defined Dr. O's approach slowly started to fade. Rather than innovating, she found herself sticking rigidly to protocol, afraid to deviate from the established playbook. Her creative problem-solving abilities, once her greatest strength, atrophied as she became increasingly cautious and risk averse.

The patients began to notice the change as well. The warmth and enthusiasm that had drawn them to her was replaced by a detached, mechanistic demeanor. They sensed her distraction and hesitation, eroding the trust and rapport that are so essential in healthcare. As Dr. O's passion for her work waned, so too did her resilience. The constant stress of trying to achieve perfection in an inherently imperfect field took a heavy toll. She found herself increasingly fatigued, withdrawn from her colleagues, and plagued by self-doubt. In the busy ER where seconds matter, Dr. O had several incidents in which her paralysis nearly cost a patient's life. All of this became too much, and she quit.

As we worked together, she began to understand how her relentless pursuit of perfection had stifled her creativity and joy, leading her down a path of burnout and disillusionment. Slowly, Dr. O learned to embrace a more balanced, compassionate approach to her work. She acknowledged that medicine, like life, is inherently imperfect, and that the true mark of a great doctor is not flawlessness, but the courage to make informed decisions, learn from mistakes, and put the well-being of patients first. This shift in mindset not only restored her love for her work, but also allowed her to rediscover the creative spark that had once defined her as a pioneering clinician.

In our relentless pursuit of success and achievement, we often fall into the trap of perfectionism—a dangerous mindset that can stifle our creativity, passion, and overall well-being. The story of Dr. O serves as a poignant reminder of the perils of this path and the transformative power of embracing a purpose-driven, creative mindset.

Perfectionism is rooted in fear—fear of failure, judgment, or not living up to unrealistic expectations. It manifests as an obsessive need for control, a tendency to fixate on flaws, and an unyielding adherence to rigid standards. While a certain level of meticulousness can be beneficial, taken to the extreme, perfectionism becomes a prison that traps us in a cycle of self-doubt, procrastination, and paralysis.

When we operate from this perfectionistic mindset, we close ourselves off from the very qualities that fuel creativity and innovation. Creativity requires a willingness to take risks, to experiment, and to embrace the messiness of the process. It thrives in an environment of curiosity, playfulness, and openness to new ideas—qualities that are antithetical to the rigid, risk-averse nature of perfectionism.

Moreover, perfectionism robs us of our sense of purpose and meaning. When we become consumed by the pursuit of an unattainable ideal, we lose sight of the deeper reasons that drove us to our chosen path in the first place. Like Dr. O, we may find ourselves going through the motions, detached from the very work that once ignited our passion and enthusiasm.

When I finally recognized how damaging my perfectionistic tendencies had become, I knew I had to make a profound shift. It wasn't easy at first to let go of those deeply ingrained habits and that nagging inner critic. But as I started to focus more on my deeper sense of purpose I found myself becoming liberated from the shackles of perfection.

The antidote to this destructive cycle lies in cultivating a purpose-driven, creative mindset. This mindset is grounded in a deep understanding of our core values and the impact we wish to have on the world around us. It is fueled by a sense of curiosity, a willingness to embrace challenges as opportunities for growth, and a commitment to continual learning and self-improvement. Ultimately, by embracing a creative, purpose-driven mindset, we unlock a path to deep fulfillment and sustained motivation.

So I encourage you, as I had to learn for myself, to let go of the pursuit of perfection and instead chase purpose and meaningful impact. It is in this space of creative freedom, untethered from unrealistic expectations, that we can truly thrive as professionals and human beings. When we operate from this mindset, we are liberated from the shackles of perfection and can fully embrace the creative process. We become more resilient in the face of setbacks, viewing them not as failures but as valuable lessons that propel us forward. We approach our work with a sense of playfulness and joy, allowing our natural creativity and problem-solving abilities to flourish.

Furthermore, a purpose-driven mindset fosters a deeper connection with our work and the people we serve. Like Dr. O's early days, when she was driven by a genuine desire to improve patient outcomes, we become more attuned to the human element of our endeavors. We approach challenges with empathy, compassion, and a commitment to making a positive impact, rather than being consumed by the need to achieve flawless results.

Ultimately, by embracing a creative, purpose-driven mindset, we unlock a path to deep fulfillment and sustained motivation. We rediscover the joy and passion that first inspired us to pursue our chosen path, and we become more resilient in the face of the inevitable challenges and setbacks that life throws our way.

So let us challenge ourselves to let go of the pursuit of perfection and instead chase purpose, embracing the messy, beautiful reality of the creative process. For it is in this space, free from the constraints of perfection, that we can truly thrive, innovate, and leave a lasting, meaningful impact on the world around us.

Nurturing Creativity in Daily Life

While the exercises and concepts discussed so far have provided a foundation for understanding and accessing your creative potential, the true key to sustaining creativity lies in nurturing it as a daily practice. Creativity is not a finite resource to be exhausted but rather a muscle that grows stronger the more you exercise it.

In our fast-paced, productivity-driven world, it's all too easy to get caught up in the relentless pursuit of checking boxes and meeting deadlines. We become so focused on the end goal that we forget to enjoy the journey itself. This is where the magic of creativity can restore balance and breathe new life into our routines.

Embracing a Beginner's Mindset

One of the greatest obstacles to nurturing creativity is the fear of failure or the belief that we must be experts to try something new. However, true creativity thrives when we approach experiences with a beginner's mindset—a willingness to be a novice, to make mistakes, and to find joy in the process of learning and exploration.

Imagine yourself as a child, unencumbered by self-judgment or the need for perfection. With unbridled curiosity, you would eagerly dive into new activities, reveling in the act of discovery and creation. Recapturing this sense of wonder and playfulness is the key to unlocking your creative potential.

Scheduling Creativity

While spontaneity has its place, intentionally carving out time for creative pursuits is crucial for nurturing your creative spirit. Just as you would schedule appointments or meetings, dedicate specific times in your calendar for engaging in creative activities, whether it's painting, writing, gardening, or any other pursuit that resonates with you.

Treat this time as sacred, free from distractions and the demands of your daily obligations. During these creative sessions, resist the urge to judge or critique your work. Instead, embrace the process and allow your mind to wander, explore, and play without restraint.

Seeking Inspiration

To keep your creativity well replenished, actively seek out sources of inspiration in your daily life. This could involve immersing yourself in nature, attending cultural events, reading books or watching films that challenge your perspectives, or engaging in thought-provoking conversations with others.

Additionally, consider joining a creative community, whether online or in person, where you can share your work, receive feedback, and draw inspiration from the creative expressions of others. Surrounding yourself with like-minded individuals can provide a supportive environment that encourages growth and experimentation.

Celebrating Small Victories

As you embark on this creative journey, celebrate each small victory and milestone along the way. Completed a new painting? Acknowledge the effort and joy that went into creating it. Wrote a short story you're proud of? Share it with a friend or family member and bask in their appreciation.

Celebrating these small victories reinforces the intrinsic rewards of creativity and fuels your motivation to continue exploring and expanding your creative horizons.

Remember, nurturing creativity is an ongoing practice, not a destination. By embracing a beginner's mindset, scheduling dedicated creative time, seeking inspiration, and celebrating your small victories, you can cultivate a lifelong relationship with your creative genius—a relationship that will enrich your personal growth, professional endeavors, and overall well-being.

Conclusion: Unleashing Your Creative Potential

In a world that often prioritizes productivity over purpose, rediscovering your creative genius is an act of rebirth—rising like a phoenix from the ashes of burnout. By redefining creativity as a limitless force that permeates every aspect of our lives, we unlock a powerful antidote to the stress and monotony that fuels burnout.

The journey toward unleashing your creative potential is not a linear path but a continuous exploration, a dance between structure and spontaneity, between discipline and play. Learning to dance with the fire and developing a rhythm that strategically contains the blaze while also allowing space for a healthy burn. Embrace the exercises and insights shared in this chapter as starting points, not endpoints. Allow them to ignite a spark within you, a flame that will continue to burn brightly as you nurture your creativity through daily practice, seek inspiration from the world around you, and celebrate the small victories that pave the way to your authentic self-expression. Remember, cultivating creativity is not an indulgence but a necessity—a fundamental aspect of living a life filled with purpose, passion, and an unwavering sense of joy.

So go forth, and embark on this transformative journey, for within the depths of your creative genius lies the key to overcoming burnout and reclaiming the vibrant, fulfilling life you deserve. This deep fulfillment and creative flow is amplified when we share it with a supportive community. In the next chapter we will learn how to attain *collective genius*.

"Creativity is intelligence having fun."

- Albert Einstein

CHAPTER 9
GATHERING AROUND THE CAMPFIRE:
FOSTERING COMMUNITY FOR COLLECTIVE RESILIENCE

Healthcare professions can be incredibly isolating. Spending so much of our time at work, especially during our early twenties when others are forming the bonds of adult friendship, having little time for hobbies or leisure activities, and having nothing to talk about but blood, gore, and suffering definitely don't make for an easy path to connection and community. Many people turn to work as a place for friendships, and it may be, but all too often this desire leads to weird boundary violations that end up doing more harm than good.

What's my solution? No surprise here, intentional connection grounded in your values and goals. Connection itself is an outcome. Being part of a group can be incredibly nourishing. It can also be draining and become one more thing on your to-do list. You need to find the right group and then commit yourself to showing up as a part of it.

The Power of Shared Experiences: Finding Your Flock in Healthcare

Having a group that has a common basis of understanding is invaluable to getting through tough days. This can be an informal text group, or a lunch bunch, or some other collection of people who understand they serve this purpose to each other. This group should be small. I'm not talking about a listserv or some Facebook group with thousands of members. This is a group of people you know personally and who already have the context needed to allow for frank conversation.

I have a group of other palliative care doctors from across the country. It is not entirely clear anymore how this little band of misfits assembled, but now we are a group and we call ourselves the PPC Spicy Peppers. Conversation in this group sticks to professional topics (not direct patient care) with occasional jaunts into silliness for the sake of levity. This group is magical for a few reasons:

- Most of us are in leadership positions and may not have suitable outlets for venting frustrations or asking vulnerable questions within our own institutions.
- We are cast across the country and in institutions of varying size, yet the commonality of our experiences is always striking and validating.
- We celebrate each other's wins. In a hyper-competitive environment like healthcare, it can be hard to say you are proud of yourself for

something. Several times in this group, someone will have won an award or gotten recognition for something and not said anything about it. Another group member will dig up that announcement and share it and celebration will commence. We have a shared understanding of how hard it is to toot your own horn, so we do it for each other. It's magic!
- We call each other on BS. This group has come to serve as a reality check for many of us. "Hey y'all, just checking if my thinking on this is good or not" kind of thing. Everyone gets in their own way sometimes and even the most mindful among us sometimes just can't see the mind trash that is clouding our vision. Having a safe space to get feedback is amazing.

An informal group like this is important. The structure of your group may look different from mine. I do strongly encourage, though, that everyone in the group realize they are in a group. Although this is informal in the sense that you don't collect dues or take minutes or anything like that, it is a structure, a container if you will. This makes it stronger than just a mental list of people you have that you can talk to about stuff. Every decision we make comes with a cost in mental load; having the group already established saves you so many decisions. Also, having the group already established encourages engagement. It's there, you might as well use it.

Now of course, like any relationship, the flock needs tending. Finding the right people and creating the right culture in the group is essential. Using the communication strategies we covered in chapter 5, you should be able to navigate this with ease. Remember, there is a period of forming, storming, and norming with every group before you get to the transforming. Oh, but when you do get there! It is really magical to have a group that gets it and loves you just as you are.

Go find your flock!

Mentorship and Peer Support: Formal and Informal Ways to Build Community

Developing a network of people who can help you find opportunities and learn is another essential community to cultivate. The importance of networking is well understood in the business world, but we have been slower to catch on in healthcare.

A mentor is someone who has gone down the path ahead of you. They know what it takes to accomplish a certain goal. For example, if you want to become a nurse practitioner, find a mentor who is a nurse practitioner to guide you on the steps you need to take to achieve that. We can also seek creative sources of mentorship as well. For example, if you want to improve your communication skills and ability to motivate patients to make lifestyle changes. You may seek a mentor in a completely different field such as marketing or conflict resolution to help you develop skills that can be adapted to the bedside.

Joining a group of people working toward a similar outcome is a great way to gain support for projects and initiatives. For example, if you are hoping to implement a family advisory council, seeking mentorship from institutions that have already implemented this is a great first step. Then reaching out to other institutions who are also in the planning and implementation phase to form a workgroup will keep everyone on task and energized compared to working on it alone. This is the idea of many of the quality improvement collaboratives and workgroups offered through national organizations. If you want to go fast, go alone. If you want to go far, go together.

Raise your hand and ask for help. Or if you are a person farther along the path, offer help to someone who asks. Being part of a community feeds our human needs for connection, significance, and growth. Connecting your actions back to your core values and strengths and attaching them to joy (all the stuff we have covered so far!) will keep you from feeling drained and ensure you feel energized by all this connection. Of course, a balance of downtime and uptime is needed. Taking time alone and in quiet reflection (remember to rest) is also very important.

Balance is the key. I'm not saying join every club and spend hours every day mentoring new nurses. Find some element of community that feels right for you at this time and commit to it.

Online communities for healthcare professionals: a guide to finding your virtual tribe.

Finding the right group

Where to even start. Today's world feels like there are endless groups on every social media platform and many online programs for clinician wellness. In "real life" there are also many groups from professional organizations to task forces to interest groups at your hospital. The things to evaluate when considering if joining a particular group aligns with your goals and values are:

1. **Mission and Purpose**: Make sure the group's mission and objectives are clearly defined and align with what you're looking for. Some groups may focus on peer support, while others might be more education- or advocacy-centered.
2. **Member Demographics**: Does the group cater specifically to women in healthcare or is it broader? Depending on your preference, you might be looking for a group that understands the unique challenges faced by women in the sector.
3. **Professional Diversity**: Healthcare is a vast field with diverse roles. Consider whether the group caters to a specific profession (e.g., nurses, doctors, therapists) or is more inclusive of various roles. A broader group might offer diverse perspectives but may not be as tailored to specific challenges.

4. **Meeting Structure**: Understand how often the group meets and the format of the meetings. Is it more of a formal presentation or a relaxed discussion? Knowing this can help you gauge if it's the kind of support environment you're seeking.
5. **Anonymity and Confidentiality**: It's essential to ensure the group respects members' privacy. If you wish to share personal experiences, you need to be confident that what's discussed remains confidential.
6. **Mentoring Opportunities**: Some groups may offer mentorship opportunities, pairing more experienced members with newer ones. If you're looking for guidance, this could be a beneficial feature.
7. **Resources and Educational Opportunities**: Check if the group offers resources, workshops, or guest speakers. These can provide valuable insights and tools to handle burnout.
8. **Values and Code of Conduct**: Look into the group's stated values and any code of conduct. This will give you a sense of the group's culture and how members are expected to treat one another.
9. **Feedback and Reviews**: Seek feedback from current or past members. They can provide insight into the group's dynamics, the benefits they've experienced, and any challenges they've encountered.

10. **Engagement Opportunities**: A community group that offers various ways to engage, such as volunteering, organizing events, or contributing to discussions, can be more fulfilling.
11. **Cost and Commitment**: Some groups might have membership fees or expect a certain level of commitment. Make sure these align with your budget and availability.
12. **Online vs. Offline**: In today's digital age, there are many online communities. Decide if you prefer in-person meetings, virtual meetings, or a blend of both.
13. **Flexibility**: Life as a healthcare worker can be unpredictable. Consider how flexible the group is regarding attendance and participation. A group that understands and accommodates the demanding schedules of healthcare professionals would be ideal.

In summary, when seeking a community group to support your thriving and sustainability, it's essential to do your research and find one that resonates with your needs, values, and goals. It might also be helpful to attend a few sessions or meetings before making a long-term commitment to ensure it's the right fit for you.

Commitment to Participation

The specifics of your commitment largely depends on the type of group and the structure. Set your intention that you seek meaningful connection while maintaining your well-being and balance.

For me, social media bears too many burdens for anything in this space to feel truly nourishing. I do know many people who find discussions on social media meaningful and greatly enjoy participating in the various groups they belong to. The problem I have with most groups on social media is that it too easily gets out of control. People are often expressing unfiltered opinions that are harmful to others and it moves too fast for anyone to really get ahold of it.

I have seen online groups work, but they work best when there is an accompanying offline relationship and foundation of values and culture. Even then, the unfiltered environment of social media sometimes allows things to run off the rails, but it is better. This makes me sad though because I think technology offers so much promise. It allows us to speak with people who are separated from us by vast distances. I have been in Zoom rooms with people I would never be able to be in a room with in real life (or not so easily anyway.)

Creating a space where healthcare professionals can gather to seek and offer support is our mission at The Recharge Studio. We aim to create a space that is inclusive and comfortable with offerings tailored to healthcare professionals. Check it out.

Being part of a group is like any relationship: a give and take. If you have selected the right group, it should not be something you dread or find painful to attend, but you do need to do the work of organizing your life so that you can attend the meetings. Prioritizing the hour (or whatever time) and committing to be fully present are your commitments to the group. Some groups have additional membership agreements such as code of conduct and group values to be upheld.

The Importance of Interdisciplinary Collaboration: Learning from Other Fields Inside and Outside of Healthcare

The healthcare field can greatly benefit from interdisciplinary collaboration that extends beyond just working with other medical professionals. By learning from experts in fields outside of healthcare, providers can gain fresh perspectives and innovative approaches to enhancing patient care and workplace well-being. For example, partnering with professionals from the hospitality industry could offer insights into creating a more patient-centered experience and improving customer service skills. Collaborating with experts in user experience design and technology could lead to developing more intuitive and user-friendly medical devices, apps, or electronic health records.

Moreover, fields like psychology, sociology, and anthropology can provide valuable knowledge about human behavior, cultural competency, and effective communication strategies. Healthcare providers could work with professionals from these disciplines to better understand the psychosocial factors influencing patients' health decisions and to develop more culturally sensitive care approaches. Engaging with experts in change management, organizational behavior, or human resources could help healthcare organizations implement systemic changes more effectively, improve workplace culture, and foster a more positive and supportive environment for staff. By embracing interdisciplinary collaboration and being open to learning from diverse fields, healthcare professionals can expand their knowledge, challenge traditional paradigms, and ultimately deliver more comprehensive and holistic care to their patients.

Wellness Events: Bringing the Healthcare Community Together for Shared Well-being

Wellness events specifically designed for healthcare professionals can play a crucial role in fostering a sense of community, providing support, and promoting overall well-being within the industry. These events offer a much-needed respite from the high-stress and demanding nature of healthcare work, allowing practitioners to recharge, connect with colleagues, and explore various aspects of personal and professional wellness. From mindfulness retreats and yoga sessions to cooking classes and outdoor adventures, wellness events can cater to diverse interests and needs, encouraging healthcare workers to prioritize their mental, physical, and emotional health.

Beyond the direct benefits to individual well-being, wellness events also serve to strengthen the broader healthcare community. They provide opportunities for professionals across different roles and specialties to come together, share experiences, and learn from one another in a relaxed and supportive environment. These connections can help reduce feelings of isolation, facilitate knowledge sharing, and foster a greater sense of camaraderie and mutual understanding within the healthcare field. Ultimately, wellness events remind healthcare workers that their own well-being is just as important as the care they provide to others, and that prioritizing self-care and community support is essential for sustainable and effective patient care.

Communities Outside of Work

Now that we fully understand the importance of being a whole human, not just a healthcare worker, we can embrace the necessity of communities outside of work. This is vital to our sustainability and thriving. While there is certainly value in socializing with coworkers to build camaraderie and rapport, having communities entirely separate from your professional life is crucial. I invite you to develop a multifaceted identity that extends far beyond your job. This may feel daunting at first, especially if you're shy or grappling with insecurities. But community is essential—we need human connection and meaningful relationships.

When I first moved to Boston, I was entirely isolated, knowing no one except my husband, kids, and new colleagues. After about six months, I recognized the need to forge local connections. I joined an eccentric but welcoming fitness group called November Project, initially attending their Harvard Stadium stair-climbing workouts without much interaction. Gradually, I met friends from all walks of life through this community. Having a space where I was simply Emma, not Dr. Jones, was profoundly nourishing. While physical exercise alone benefits mental health, exercising within a supportive community amplifies the magic.

Later, when I hit a deeper burnout phase, I found solace in a yoga studio's community. Starting with Yin Yoga classes recommended for my chronic back pain, I unexpectedly discovered a sanctuary. On difficult days, I'd show up on my mat, sometimes just lying face-down, crying, or even falling during poses. But I kept returning, drawn by the nonjudgmental space and the simple act of practice alongside others on a similar journey.

Ultimately, I embarked on a 200-hour yoga teacher training, a transformative experience that introduced me to a profound sense of community—the "sangha." Despite our diverse backgrounds, we were united by a shared commitment to growth and self-discovery. As one fellow student remarked, "I don't know what you do, if you're married, or where you're from, but I know your heart." This heart-connection reminded me that I am so much more than my profession, and that I have inherent worth beyond any accomplishments.

I encourage you to find your own nourishing community, a space that speaks to your soul. It may be a book club, a neighborhood group, or any activity that aligns with your interests and values. Investing energy into these connections can feel like added work when you're already depleted, but it is energy well spent. Having a supportive network means having help and shared burdens when times are tough—whether through tangible assistance or simply being surrounded by positivity and light without uttering a word. Cultivating communities is an essential part of the phoenix blueprint, allowing you to rise resiliently from the ashes of burnout. Within these empathetic embraces, you can nurture the fullness of your identity, replenish your spirit, and continuously reignite the radiant flame that fuels your vital work.

Your Rolodex

Remember the old school Rolodex? For those of you too young to remember, it is a desk accessory very popular in the pre-digital age. It consists of a stack of cards with holes in them all bound together on a circular center wheel so you can dial through all your contacts by rolling the wheel. Picture a doughnut made of paper that can make calls, or, better yet, imagine if LinkedIn had a baby with a lazy Susan.

I never actually had a Rolodex myself. My first attending job I did have a desk, so it would have been the perfect moment to break out this wonder of office supply sophistication. But by that point it was 2006 and I got a Blackberry instead. But a senior member of my practice had one. She had been working on that thing since the 1960s and boy did it have some goodies. One day sitting in her office, I flipped through, and I realized that these weren't just contacts—each card represented a lifeline, a potential mentor, a friend, or a colleague to lean on. I now realized how she knew the right person to call for any problem. The key piece that took me a bit longer to realize was that this treasure trove of contacts didn't happen by accident. There was intention behind each and every card. Each card stood as a reminder of a relationship that had been carefully cultivated.

Funny aside—did you know the word "Rolodex" is a portmanteau, a combination of "rolling" and "index"? I share this tidbit as an entry point to one of my small joys in life –the delightful art of the portmanteau. These linguistic blind dates have an uncanny knack for merging two perfectly respectable words into something bizarrely entertaining.

When "glamour" had a wild night out with "camping," they shamelessly woke up as "glamping"—because why shouldn't you sleep under the stars with a crystal chandelier dangling from your tent's ceiling? And can you imagine if "sloths" ever decided to run a "marathon"? I suspect they'd invent the "slothon"—a fourteen-year race with mandatory sloth-sized snack breaks every three minutes. Now that's an endurance event I could get behind!

Portmanteaus bring me such simple, quirky delight. There's something playfully subversive about smashing two words together and letting the awkward lovechild word take on a whimsical life of its own. I'd be lost without nonsensically joyful jumbles like "hangry," "framily," and of course, the immortal "brunch" to enliven my vocabulary.

Okay, back to work—who would be in your Rolodex?

Exercise: Crafting Your Community Rolodex

Objective: To create an organized, intentional list of contacts from various facets of your life to foster community, support, and collaboration.

Materials Needed: A journal/notebook, pen, digital device (optional for digital Rolodex creation)

Steps:

1. Categorize Your Community:

- Begin by dividing your Rolodex into categories. Some examples could be: Professional Contacts, Personal Friends, Inspirational Individuals, Mentors/Mentees, Activity Partners (e.g., gym buddies, book club members), and Service Providers (e.g., doctor, therapist, coach).

2. Reflect and List:

- Under each category, reflect on your current network. Who do you know? Who do you wish to know better? Who plays a pivotal role in certain areas of your life?
- Begin listing names under each category, starting with those you already know.

3. Set Intentions:

- For each individual, write a sentence or two about the nature of your relationship, and more importantly, your intention for its future. For instance: "Jane—Gym buddy. Plan to collaborate on a community fitness event."

4. Mind the Gaps:

- Once you've listed existing contacts, identify gaps in your network. Are there types of individuals or professionals you wish to connect with but haven't yet?

5. Action Steps for Connection:

- For those gaps, write actionable steps on how you intend to connect with such individuals or groups. For example, if you lack a mentor in your professional life, an action step could be: "Attend two educational webinars this month and reach out for networking."

6. Maintain and Nurture:

- Allocate a section for "Rolodex Rituals." These are monthly/quarterly actions you'll take to nurture these connections. This could include sending a catch-up email, scheduling a coffee chat, or sharing a resource.

7. Diversify Your Rolodex:

- Reflect on the diversity of your network. A diverse network exposes you to various perspectives and learning opportunities. Consider age, background, industry, experience, etc. Are there voices or perspectives missing?

8. Digital Adaptation (Optional):

- If you're more digitally inclined, consider translating this exercise to a digital platform. There are numerous apps and platforms designed to manage and nurture networks.

9. Review and Revise:

- Schedule quarterly "Rolodex Reviews" in your calendar. Revisit your list, note changes, celebrate new connections, and reflect on relationships that have deepened or shifted.

10. Engage:

- Every month, randomly select a few contacts from your Rolodex to reach out to. It could be a simple "Hello," sharing an article of interest, or suggesting a meet-up.

11. Debrief:

- Reflect on how actively fostering and attending to your community network feels. Recognize that relationships are two-way streets, and that genuine, mutual effort is the foundation for a thriving community.

Conclusion

Throughout this chapter, we have explored the vital role that community plays in sustaining wellness for healthcare professionals. In the face of intense demands, isolation, and the potential for burnout, building meaningful connections is not just a nice-to-have, but a necessity—an essential part of the phoenix blueprint for rising strong from the ashes of a healthcare system in crisis.

Whether it's an informal group text with colleagues who truly understand the challenges you face, a mentorship relationship that guides your professional growth, an online forum where you find your virtual tribe, or an interdisciplinary collaboration that expands your perspectives—community provides validation, support, and a safe space to be vulnerable. It offers celebration of your wins, a reality check when needed, and opportunities to pay it forward by nurturing others. Beyond the workplace, cultivating communities through shared interests, values, or causes nourishes the whole human that you are beyond your healthcare role. In community is where the full radiance of your spirit can ignite!

Investing time and energy into fostering these supportive networks may feel daunting amid your already overwhelming responsibilities. But recognize that this is an investment in your longevity and passion for your vital work. These communities will prop you up and propel you forward. The dividends it pays in sustaining your resilience, reigniting your purpose, and preventing burnout are immeasurable. So take that first step to find your flock—those kindred spirits who uplift you and with whom you can show up authentically. The transformative power of true community is profound, and within its empathetic embrace, you can thrive.

But these stories don't mean anything when you've got no one to tell them to…

– "The Story," Brandi Carlile

CHAPTER 10
RISING FROM THE ASHES:
EMBRACING THE JOURNEY OF TRANSFORMATION

Some days the rug just gets pulled out from under you. It happens to everyone.

I have bad news, there is no amount of meditation or self-love or values-based decision-making that can prevent bad things from happening. Something is going to happen. I'm not necessarily talking about big life circumstances here (although those will inevitably happen too). I want you to be prepared for the little things that are really insignificant but can so easily sweep us away.

It will most likely take you by surprise. Here are a few moments in my life recently that had this effect.

- Receiving a text from a coworker that I have a difficult relationship with, which sent me into a spiral regretting every life choice I have ever made.

- Crashing into another car as I pulled out of my driveway (directly onto a very busy intersection), leading me to believe I am the worst driver that has ever lived.
- Having a fight with my teenager about…anything (they can really push your buttons), bringing up many old wounds from my own teenage years and tempting me to react more harshly than necessary.

You get it, this formula will not make every day roses. What it will do is give you the power to get back on your feet as quickly as possible. Fall back to the foundations, rest and restore, shore up any boundaries that may have faltered, get curious about what you are feeling and where it is showing up physically. And then just hold that for a minute, let it be what it is. Offer yourself compassion and tenderness. Take a breath. With all the work you have done, you know how it feels to trust yourself. You know how it feels to say "it will be okay" even when you have no idea how or when. Just for a moment, hold it all. Breath in, breath out. You got this!

This journey is one that ebbs and flows and moves forward and back because that's life. I've presented this to you as a somewhat linear path, but it's not like once you reach the end you are done. Some of the earlier steps become more automatic as your skills increase and you have more capacity to advocate and serve as a stand for others.

The Phoenix Blueprint: Reclaiming Your Light Amid the Flames

In this book, we have explored the step-by-step *Phoenix Blueprint*—a holistic framework for how healthcare workers can reclaim their inner light and flourish, even amid the consuming flames of burnout. We began by acknowledging the pervasive epidemic of burnout plaguing the healthcare system, where self-sacrifice and overwork have become the norm. Many of us have even found ourselves secretly wishing for a serious health diagnosis, just to have an "excuse" to finally rest.

Blueprint for Thriving Amid Burnout:

1. Rest

- Prioritize rest, recuperation, and rejuvenation to recharge physical, mental, and emotional resources.

2. Self-Study

- Engage in reflection and self-examination to understand the root causes of burnout.

3. Establish Healthy Boundaries

- Set clear boundaries to protect physical, mental, and emotional well-being.

4. Effective Communication

- Cultivate open and honest communication with colleagues, loved ones, and support systems.

5. Shine for Others

- Find ways to contribute and make a positive impact, tapping into a sense of purpose.

6. Advocacy

- Advocate for systemic changes to address the societal and organizational factors contributing to burnout.

7. Creativity

- Redefine creativity beyond just artistic pursuits, and actively engage in creative expression to unlock joy and power.
- Use creativity in problem-solving, communication, and daily tasks.

8. Community

- Recognize the vital role of community in supporting wellness and recovery.
- Foster meaningful connections and share stories with others to find resonance and belonging.

When you follow the blueprint and incorporate these interconnected elements, you will begin to navigate the challenges of burnout and cultivate sustainable well-being. My hope is that you take these lessons with you, far beyond the time you spend reading this book. Embracing this as a journey, one whose map you may not be fully able to see yet, is the key. Develop your map by planning using the exercises in this chapter. But more importantly, develop your map-making skills. Know that when life comes at you, you have what it takes to pivot and draw a new map. This is the heart of the firefighter and the phoenix. Planning for known contingencies and ready to rise when the fire inevitably arrives.

Developing emotional agility: adapting to the ups and downs of the healthcare profession.

Navigating the ups and downs inherent in healthcare work requires a level of emotional agility. As professionals tasked with caring for others in their most vulnerable moments, we are constantly exposed to a range of intense emotions—from the profound joy of witnessing a patient's recovery, to the deep sorrow of loss. Developing the ability to acknowledge, process, and adaptively respond to these emotional experiences is crucial for sustaining wellness.

At the core of emotional agility is self-awareness. Healthcare providers must take the time for introspection, to understand their own emotional triggers, thought patterns, and habitual reactions. With this self-knowledge, one can learn to "walk the middle path"—neither suppressing difficult emotions nor becoming overwhelmed by them. Practices like mindfulness, journaling, and seeking counseling can cultivate this self-awareness.

Equally important is the ability to shift perspectives. When facing a particularly challenging situation, the ability to step back and consider alternative viewpoints can prevent emotional reactivity. Perhaps there is useful wisdom to glean from the experience, or an opportunity to extend compassion—not just to the patient, but to oneself as the caregiver. Developing cognitive flexibility allows us to respond, rather than merely react.

Ultimately, emotional agility is about holding space for the full spectrum of human emotion, while refusing to be defined or debilitated by any single feeling. It's about learning to "surf the waves" of experiences—riding the highs with gratitude, weathering the lows with resilience, and recognizing that all states, positive or negative, are inherently temporary. With practice, healthcare professionals can cultivate this capacity, ensuring their own wellbeing even as they pour their hearts into the sacred work of caring for others. The Phoenix Blueprint gives you all the core skills you need to become emotionally agile and to model these skills for others.

Lifelong learning: Continuing education as a tool for growth and engagement.

We all know we need to keep up with the latest advancements in medical science. Yearly CME or CEU requirements can begin to feel like another box to be checked on our endless to-do lists. But lifelong learning isn't just about keeping up; it's about engagement, rekindling passion, and redefining our professional narratives. Dive in, embrace the continuous journey, and let every new lesson reignite the curious flame within.

When you commit to maintaining a beginner's mind and embracing the love of learning, you will see how ongoing learning is essential to our survival. If you aren't growing, you are dying (or at least stagnant), there is no such thing as just staying in place. The key is taking ownership over your learning. Yes, there will always be those annual education things you have to click through; get over it and just do it. I mean taking ownership of what direction you want to learn and grow in overall. Is there a niche expertise within your field you are interested in? Is there a topic outside of healthcare you are interested in learning more about? Maybe at this point, the thing you are most committed to learning more about is yourself. All of these are great targets that you can use to set intentions for your lifelong learning plan.

The role of gratitude in resilience: harnessing the power of thankfulness.

Gratitude is the magic special sauce that makes you invincible to burnout for the long haul. Being grateful for what you have and living in a state of wonder and awe for everything is really the highest achievement of all this personal growth business. Building up your gratitude muscle is one of the best things you can do to sustain your resilience over time. Right now, you are feeling great because you just read this book and did some of the exercises. You probably learned a few things about yourself and maybe have made a few changes to your habits. That is all wonderful and you will see positive impacts in your life. But the truth is that knowledge fades and the excitement you feel now for all these new habits will get challenged as life marches on. Gratitude is my key to maintaining the unbreakable core.

There is a Japanese parable about two dogs that illustrates how gratitude and perception can have such an amazing impact on our experiences.

> *Once upon a time, a man found two dogs. Wanting to know more about each dog's nature, he decided to conduct an experiment.*
>
> *He locked the first dog in a room full of mirrors for several hours. The dog, seeing only reflections of himself everywhere, grew to think there were many dogs around. Feeling threatened, he barked and growled continuously, and by the end of the day, he was exhausted and angry.*
>
> *The next day, the man locked the second dog in the same room. This dog, upon seeing his reflection everywhere, thought he was in a room full of friendly dogs. He wagged his tail, yipped in joy, and by the end of the day, he emerged happy and invigorated.*

The room is the same, but the dogs had different experiences based on their perspectives. This tale illustrates that our perception of the world around us shapes our experiences. Approaching life with gratitude and positivity, even in repetitive or familiar circumstances, can change our entire experience.

If we want to be in happy dog mode most of the time, we need to cultivate gratitude so much that it becomes automatic.

Gratitude needs to be a practice. We can't just "feel grateful" or have "an attitude of gratitude," we need to have a consistent practice. Just like our biceps don't get stronger by reading about bicep curls, you have to actually do the reps. If our goal is to experience gratitude more frequently and easily, we need to practice "doing" gratitude. What does it mean to "do" gratitude? It can be a lot of things. It can be a simple morning practice of listing things you are thankful for. Or a journal where you write things you are thankful for. It can be the habit of taking a few minutes in the shower each morning to visualize or some app that prompts you to list your top three things every day.

The point is less about the specific thing you do and more so that you do it consistently. That's the thing about practice. You get good at the things you practice. And being good at gratitude is a very valuable life skill.

Daily Gratitude Practices for Healthcare Professionals

1. Morning Grounding (5 minutes)

- **Breathing:** Start your day by taking five deep breaths. Inhale positivity and exhale negativity.

- **Affirmation:** Repeat a gratitude-focused affirmation. For instance: "Today, I am grateful for the opportunity to heal, to care, and to make a difference."

2. Gratitude Journal (10 minutes)

- **Reflection:** At the end of your workday or before bed, set aside time to reflect on your day.
- **List-making:** In a dedicated journal, jot down three things you're grateful for from the day. These could be related to your work, patients, colleagues, or personal life. They can be big or small moments.
- **Elaboration:** For one of the items on your list, elaborate on why it was significant. How did it make you feel? Why was it impactful?

3. Gratitude Object (Throughout the day)

- Choose a small object—it could be a pendant, ring, bracelet, or even a pocket-sized stone.
- Every time you touch or see this object throughout the day, pause for a moment to think of something you're grateful for. It can act as a reminder amid the hustle of the day.

4. Patient Appreciation (Once a day)

- Select one patient you interacted with during the day and mentally send them positive energy or wishes. It's a way to extend gratitude for the trust and relationship you share.

5. Weekly Reflection (15 minutes, once a week)

- At the end of the week, review your journal entries.
- Reflect on the recurring themes or moments that brought you the most joy.
- Celebrate the connections, learnings, and challenges of the week. Recognize your growth and resilience and be grateful for the journey.

Tips for Success:

- Consistency is key. Even if some days feel harder than others, sticking to the practice will help engrain gratitude into your daily routine.
- Share the practice with a colleague or friend. Having an accountability partner can provide motivation and an opportunity to share and discuss your gratitude moments.

Over time, this daily practice will not only strengthen your gratitude muscles but also foster a positive mindset that can help you navigate the demands and challenges of the healthcare profession.

Embracing Change: Strategies for Navigating Transitions in Your Career and Personal Life

Change is everywhere. Trying to resist change is like trying not to breathe. One of the mantras I adopted during my yoga teacher training is "Not needing things to change, and knowing they can't stay the same." Life is ephemeral and fleeting. We can never take the same breath twice.

Being good at change is another amazing life skill. Adopting the mindset that everything is going to change, and your job is to flow will help you immensely in the days, weeks, and years to come. Everyone is clamoring for massive changes in the US healthcare system. We all know that this system is broken, and things need to be fixed. The thing is that even changes that are moving in an overall positive direction or toward things you want can be challenging if you have a poor mindset.

So what does it mean to have a change-positive mindset? For me, my two biggest mindset shifts that got me to loving change instead of fearing it were curiosity and possibility. I am curious about what is to come, and I see the unknown as a series of infinite possibilities. Now when I say "what if," it becomes a game to see how many things I can think of and how amazing things might be, instead of worrying about losing something you currently have.

Here are a few other ways to stay change-positive and see change as an opportunity, not a threat!

1. **Growth Through Adversity:** Understanding that challenges and changes often lead to personal and professional growth. Change pushes us out of our comfort zones, forcing us to adapt and grow.
2. **Opportunity in the Unknown:** Viewing change as a chance to learn something new, to re-evaluate

old methods, or to innovate. Instead of seeing the uncertainty that comes with change as a negative, it's viewed as a space filled with potential.
3. **Flexibility:** Being willing to pivot when necessary. This involves not holding too rigidly to one way of thinking or doing things and being open to alternative approaches.
4. **Active Engagement:** Instead of being a passive recipient of change, actively engage with it. This might mean seeking out new training, asking questions, or brainstorming solutions.
5. **Resilience:** Building the emotional and mental capacity to cope with change, even when it's unexpected or challenging. This also involves the ability to bounce back from setbacks.
6. **Positive Framing:** This is the act of interpreting and thinking about change in a way that finds positive aspects or outcomes, even in challenging situations.
7. **Seeking Support:** Recognizing that it's okay to seek help or collaborate with others when navigating change. This can be in the form of mentors, colleagues, friends, or professionals.
8. **Continuous Learning:** Viewing life as a continuous journey of learning. Change often brings new information, techniques, and perspectives to light. A change-positive mindset involves being a lifelong learner.

9. **Accepting Impermanence:** Recognizing that most situations, both good and bad, are temporary. This can provide comfort during tough transitions and encourage appreciation during positive moments.
10. **Being Proactive:** Instead of waiting for change to happen, those with a change-positive mindset often anticipate and prepare for change, positioning themselves to handle it effectively.

In essence, a change-positive mindset shifts the narrative from "change is happening to me" to "change is happening, and I can navigate it successfully." For professions that are constantly evolving, like healthcare, technology, and business, fostering a change-positive mindset can be invaluable in staying updated, relevant, and effective in one's role.

Maintaining Balance: Ongoing Strategies for Work-life Integration

Everything you have learned so far has equipped you to find the work-life integration strategy that is right for you. Before you put this book down and rush back into your busy life, I want you to take a few minutes to solidify your ideas and make an action plan you can return to when things are going off the rails. The action plan worksheet can also be found on our website as a free download. Use a digital copy to play around with and make your map, then print it out so you can reference it often.

Work-Life Integration Action Plan

1. Reflection:

Visualize your ideal work-life integration. How does it look and feel?

2. Current State Analysis:

Where are you currently with your work-life integration? What's working and what isn't?

- **Strengths:** *What aspects of your current work-life integration are effective and satisfying?*
- **Areas for Improvement:** *What challenges are you currently facing in achieving the desired integration?*

3. Priority Setting:

List the key areas of your life and rank them in terms of current importance.

For example: Work, Family, Health, Personal Development, Socializing, Hobbies, etc.

4. Goal Setting:

Define specific goals for improving work-life integration.

For example: "Spend quality time with family at least three evenings a week."

5. Boundaries & Time Management:

How will you set clear boundaries and manage your time to achieve these goals?

- **Boundaries:** *Examples: No work emails after 8 p.m., weekend tech detox, etc.*
- **Time Management Strategies:** *Examples: Use of productivity tools, delegation, blocking time for self-care, etc.*

6. Support System:

Identify individuals or groups that can support you in achieving work-life integration.

For example: Family members understanding work schedules, a mentor guiding you, etc.

7. Potential Roadblocks:

What obstacles might prevent you from achieving your desired work-life integration? How will you overcome them?

8. Self-Care & Rejuvenation:

List activities or practices that rejuvenate you and make a concrete plan for incorporating them into your routine.

Examples:

- *Practice meditation each morning immediately when I wake up for five minutes.*

- *Take a walk outside for ten minutes every day after eating lunch.*
- *Attend yoga class at x studio on Wednesday nights at 6 p.m.*
- *Attend book club at y bookstore every third Thursday of the month (and read for twenty minutes per day)*

9. Review and Adjust:

Set periodic review dates to assess your progress and adjust your plan as necessary.

For example: Monthly check-ins, quarterly reviews, etc.

- **Next Review Date: _____**

_____

10. Affirmation:

Craft a personal affirmation related to work-life integration that you can refer to during challenging times. Choose one or more of the ones here and modify to fit your unique goals and vision. Write this personal affirmation on a notecard or in your journal so that you can reflect on it daily.

Affirmations

1. **Inner Strength:** "I possess the strength and courage to overcome any challenges that come my way."

2. **Self-Worth:** "I am deserving of love, kindness, and respect."
3. **Potential:** "Every day, I unlock more of my potential and embrace the opportunities that arise."
4. **Positivity:** "I radiate positivity and attract positive experiences into my life."
5. **Healing:** "Every breath I take is a step toward healing and renewal."
6. **Present Moment:** "I am fully present in this moment, embracing life as it unfolds."
7. **Self-Belief:** "I believe in myself and trust in my abilities to succeed."
8. **Growth:** "Every experience in my life helps me grow and evolve."
9. **Balance**: "I gracefully balance my professional responsibilities with my personal needs and joys."
10. **Self-Compassion:** "I am gentle with myself, understanding that progress is made step by step."
11. **Endurance:** "Challenges only make me stronger and more resilient."
12. **Abundance:** "Abundance flows freely to me in all areas of my life."
13. **Harmony:** "I am in harmony with the universe and everything in it."
14. **Gratitude:** "I am deeply thankful for the abundance in my life and the love that surrounds me."

15. **Connection:** "I am connected with the world around me, drawing strength and giving love."
16. **Compassion**: "Through my hands and heart, I offer compassion and healing to every life I touch."
17. **Resilience**: "Even in the most challenging shifts, I am resilient, grounded, and unwavering in my commitment."
18. **Empowerment**: "I am a beacon of strength and inspiration for both my patients and peers."
19. **Self-care**: "I prioritize my own well-being, knowing that to care for others, I must first care for myself."
20. **Validation**: "Every effort I make, seen or unseen, contributes profoundly to the wellness of others."
21. **Growth**: "Each day in healthcare sharpens my skills, deepens my empathy, and expands my capacity to love."
22. **Balance**: "I gracefully balance my professional responsibilities with my personal needs and joys."
23. **Confidence**: "I trust my knowledge, intuition, and experience. I make decisions with confidence and clarity."
24. **Purpose**: "I am here for a purpose. Every day, I make a difference in the world of healthcare."
25. **Unity**: "I am part of a powerful community of women in healthcare, and together, we uplift and support one another."

26. **Mindfulness**: "Amid the chaos, I find moments of stillness and peace, grounding myself in the present."
27. **Recognition**: "I acknowledge and honor the sacrifices I make and celebrate the victories, big and small."
28. **Restoration**: "I allow myself moments of rest and rejuvenation, understanding they're essential for my journey."
29. **Boundaries**: "I set and respect boundaries, ensuring my energy is preserved and directed where it's most needed."
30. **Legacy**: "Every step I take in healthcare contributes to a legacy of healing, empowerment, and hope."

CONCLUSION

The Phoenix Blueprint has equipped you with a comprehensive set of tools and strategies to navigate the challenges of burnout and reclaim your inner light. Remember, this is a journey—one with ebbs and flows, triumphs and setbacks. Trust that the foundations you have built will serve as your guiding map, empowering you to adapt and respond effectively when life inevitably throws you curveballs.

Transformation requires the phoenix to surrender to the fire, allowing its old self to be destroyed so a new form can rise. Every act of creation is also an act of destruction. You have the strength and resilience of the phoenix within you. Trust in this power as you walk bravely through the firestorm of the healthcare profession. Though the path ahead may seem uncertain, know that you have everything you need to rise from the ashes, shining brighter than before. This is your birthright—to transmute adversity into growth, and to be a beacon of hope for all those you serve. So go forth, with unwavering courage and compassion, and fulfill your highest calling.

"Embrace uncertainty. Some of the most beautiful chapters in our lives won't have a title until much later."

- Bob Goff

REFERENCES

Introduction

Berwick, D. M., Nolan, T. W., & Whittington, J. (2008). The triple aim: Care, health, and cost. Health Affairs (Millwood), 27(3), 759-769. https://doi.org/10.1377/hlthaff.27.3.759

Institute for Healthcare Improvement. (2022). Quintuple Aim: Why expand beyond the Triple Aim? https://www.ihi.org/insights/quintuple-aim-why-expand-beyond-triple-aim

Chapter 1

Addressing Health Worker Burnout. The U.S. Surgeon General's Advisory on Building a Thriving Health Workforce. https://www.hhs.gov/surgeongeneral/priorities/health-worker-burnout/index.html

AAMC. (2021). 2021 Workforce Projections. https://www.aamc.org

American Association of Colleges of Nursing. (2022). 2022 Student Enrollment Data. https://www.aacnnursing.org

Auerbach, D. I., Buerhaus, P. I., & Staiger, D. O. (2022). A worrisome drop in the number of young nurses. Health Affairs Forefront.
https://doi.org/10.1377/forefront.20220412.311784

Beecroft, P. C., Dorey, F., & Wenten, M. (2008). Turnover intention in new graduate nurses: A multivariate analysis. Journal of Advanced Nursing, 62(1), 41-52.
https://doi.org/10.1111/j.1365-2648.2007.04570.x

Diener, E., Wirtz, D., Tov, W., Kim-Prieto, C., Choi, D., Oishi, S., & Biswas-Diener, R. (2010). New well-being measures: Short scales to assess flourishing and positive and negative feelings. Social Indicators Research, 97(2), 143-156. https://doi.org/10.1007/s11205-009-9493-

Dyrbye, L. N., Thomas, M. R., Massie, F. S., Power, D. V., Eacker, A., Harper, W., Durning, S., Moutier, C., Szydlo, D. W., Novotny, P. J., Sloan, J. A., & Shanafelt, T. D. (2008). Burnout and suicidal ideation among U.S. medical students. Annals of Internal Medicine, 149(5), 334-341.
https://doi.org/10.7326/0003-4819-149-5-200809020-00008

Healthcare Workforce Analytics. (2022). 2022 Nursing Shortage Projections.
https://bhw.hrsa.gov/sites/default/files/bureau-health-workforce/data-research/nursing-projections-factsheet.pdf

Incredible Health. (2022). 2022 Nurse Retention Report. https://www.incrediblehealth.com

Maslach, C., Jackson, S. E., & Leiter, M. P. (1996). Maslach Burnout Inventory (3rd ed.). Consulting Psychologists Press.

Physicians Foundation. (2023). 2023 Survey of America's Physicians: COVID-19 Impact Edition. https://www.physiciansfoundation.org

Shanafelt, T. D., Dyrbye, L. N., West, C. P., Sinsky, C. A., & Trockel, M. T. (2023). Career plans of US physicians after the first 2 years of the COVID-19 pandemic. Mayo Clinic Proceedings, 98(11), 9-1640. https://doi.org/10.1016/j.mayocp.2023.07.002

Tawfik, D. S., Profit, J., Morgenthaler, T. I., Satele, D. V., Sinsky, C. A., Dyrbye, L. N., Tutty, M. A., West, C. P., & Shanafelt, T. D. (2018). Physician burnout, well-being, and work unit safety grades in relationship to reported medical errors. Mayo Clinic Proceedings, 93(11), 1571-1580. https://doi.org/10.1016/j.mayocp.2018.05.014

Chapter 2

Brown, B. (2017). Rising strong: How the ability to reset transforms the way we live, love, parent, and lead. Random House.

Carroll, B., Jr., Pugh, M., & Oppenheimer, J. (Writers), & Asher, W. (Director). (1952, September 15). Job switching [Television series episode]. In J. Oppenheimer (Executive

Producer), I Love Lucy. Desilu Productions. https://youtu.be/K3axU2b0dDk

Getting Things Done (n.d.). https://gettingthingsdone.com/

Indistractible (n.d.). https://www.nirandfar.com/indistractable/

Neff, K. (n.d.). Self-compassion. https://self-compassion.org/

Patanjali. (n.d.). Yoga Sutras of Patanjali.

Walker, M. (2017). Why we sleep: Unlocking the power of sleep and dreams. Scribner.

Chapter 3

Allen, D. (2001). Getting things done: The art of stress-free productivity. Penguin.

Byron Katie. (n.d.). https://thework.com/

Covey, S. R. (2004). The 7 habits of highly effective people: Powerful lessons in personal change. Free Press.

Daily Stoic. (n.d.). https://dailystoic.com/

Hawkins, D. R. (2012). Letting go: The pathway of surrender. Hay House.

Neff, K. D. (2021). Fierce self-compassion: How women can harness kindness to speak up, claim their power, and thrive. HarperCollins.

VIA Institute on Character. (n.d.). VIA character strengths survey & character reports.
https://www.viacharacter.org/

Chapter 4

Nelson, P. (1993). Autobiography in five short chapters. In B. Furman (Ed.), There's a hole in my sidewalk: The romance of self-discovery (p. 1). Beyond Words Publishing.

Positivity Psychology. (n.d.). How to set healthy boundaries: 10 examples + PDF worksheets.
https://positivepsychology.com/great-self-care-setting-healthy-boundaries/

Psychology Today. (2023, April 20). Why people-pleasing isn't pleasing anyone.
https://www.psychologytoday.com/intl/blog/the-now/202304/why-people-pleasing-isnt-pleasing-anyone

Tawwab, N. G. (2021). Set boundaries, find peace: A guide to reclaiming yourself. TarcherPerigee.

Waters, A. (2017). Coming to my senses: The making of a counterculture cook. Clarkson Potter.

Chapter 5

Psychology Today. (2021, November 21). Ho'oponopono: To Make Things Right.
https://www.psychologytoday.com/us/blog/the-time-cure/202111/hooponopono-to-make-things-right

Rosenberg, M. B. (2015). Nonviolent communication: A language of life (3rd ed.). PuddleDancer Press.

Rumi, J. (2004). The essential Rumi (C. Barks, Trans.). HarperOne.

Salzberg, S. (2002). Lovingkindness: The revolutionary art of happiness. Shambhala.

Chapter 6

Capodagli, B., & Jackson, L. (2007). The Disney way: Harnessing the management secrets of Disney in your company. McGraw-Hill.

Fredrickson, B. (2001). The role of positive emotions in positive psychology: The broaden-and-build theory of positive emotions. American Psychologist, 56(3), 218-226. https://doi.org/10.1037/0003-066x.56.3.218

Goleman, D. (2017). What makes a leader? Harvard Business Review Press.

Liker, J. K., & Hoseus, M. (2008). Toyota culture: The heart and soul of the Toyota way. McGraw-Hill.

Chapter 7

Lorna Breen Foundation. (n.d.). https://drlornabreen.org/

Walrond, K. (2021). The Lightmaker's Manifesto: How to work for change without losing your joy. Broadleaf Books.

Chapter 8

Brown, B. (2021). Atlas of the heart. Penguin Random House.

Csikszentmihalyi, M., & Nakamura, J. (2002). The concept of flow. In C. R. Snyder & S. J. Lopez (Eds.), Handbook of positive psychology (pp. 89-105). Oxford University Press.

Johnson, M. K. (2020). Joy: A review of the literature and suggestions for future directions. The Journal of Positive Psychology, 15(1), 5-24. https://doi.org/10.1080/17439760.2019.1685571

Nakamura, J., & Csikszentmihalyi, M. (2009). Flow theory and research. In S. J. Lopez & C. R. Snyder (Eds.), Oxford handbook of positive psychology (2nd ed., pp. 195-206). Oxford University Press.

Sawyer, K. (2007). Group genius: The creative power of collaboration. Basic Books.

Chapter 9

Brown, B. (2012). Daring greatly: How the courage to be vulnerable transforms the way we live, love, parent, and lead. Gotham Books.

Lieberman, M. D. (2013). Social: Why our brains are wired to connect. Crown.

November Project. (n.d.). https://november-project.com/

Chapter 10

Clear, J. (2018). Atomic habits: An easy & proven way to build good habits & break bad ones. Avery.

David, S. (2016). Emotional agility: Get unstuck, embrace change, and thrive in work and life. Avery.

Seligman, M. E. P. (2011). Flourish: A visionary new understanding of happiness and well-being. Free Press.

Made in the USA
Middletown, DE
15 October 2024

62676122R00156